D1357231

Mala's Cat

Mala's Cat

MALA KACENBERG

MICHAEL  JOSEPH

MICHAEL JOSEPH

UK | USA | Canada | Ireland | Australia
India | New Zealand | South Africa

Michael Joseph is part of the Penguin Random House group of companies
whose addresses can be found at global.penguinrandomhouse.com.

Penguin
Random House
UK

First published 2022

001

Copyright © Mala Kacenberg, 2022

The moral right of the author has been asserted

Set in 13.5/16 pt Garamond MT Std
Typeset by Jouve (UK), Milton Keynes
Printed and bound in Great Britain by Clays Ltd, Elcograf S.p.A.

The authorized representative in the EEA is Penguin Random House Ireland,
Morrison Chambers, 32 Nassau Street, Dublin D02 YH68

A CIP catalogue record for this book is available from the British Library

HARDBACK ISBN: 978–0–241–50365–2

www.greenpenguin.co.uk

In Memory of:

my dear parents, Yitzchak and Frimchy Szorer and my
grandparents who all instilled in me enough religious
knowledge to sustain me throughout the war;

my older sister Balla, whom I adored and
always looked to for guidance;

my only brother Yechiel Gershon, so brutally
murdered right at my feet;

my younger sister Esther, so bright and mature,
who was only thirteen years old when she,
too, was ruthlessly murdered;

my sweet little sisters Kresele and Surele, as golden as
their hairlocks and far too young to understand what
was happening and for whom I begged for food daily;

my younger sisters Freidele and Devoirele, who
died so very young even before the ravages
of war had commenced;

my dear uncles, aunts and cousins and so many
numerous friends, whose loss I shall always
feel and whose love I shall always remember;

the six million Jewish martyrs, who were
brutally murdered by the Germans.

Dedicated to:

my dear husband for his encouragement and
forbearance in sharing my burden of the
tragic past, for his patience and understanding
whilst I recorded these painful memories and
together with whom, with *Hashem*'s help, I was
able to rebuild a wonderful Jewish family;

our wonderful children and grandchildren –
may they continue to carry forward
the torch of their heritage.

Amen

Table of Contents

BOOK THREE

Amid the Enemy

BOOK FOUR

Return to Poland

BOOK FIVE

A New Life

Preface

I was only twelve-and-a-half years old when the shadow of the Third Reich fell across Europe. As the nightmare of the German invasion of my defenceless country began, I was more concerned with my schoolbooks and my family and friends than with the ramifications of war. I could not even begin to imagine the extent of the horrors that were soon to follow.

I was by nature a very contented child and enjoyed my early years of life immensely. In those sunny days of my childhood, I was still sheltered from the dreadful fears by my dear parents and did not know what catastrophe was going to befall the Jewish people and my family.

The passage of time since those dreadful days does not blur the images of the depths to which humanity can sink. They remain indelibly and brutally engraved in my brain. And yet, because of the enormity of the crimes, if they are to be remembered at all, I must record mid-twentieth-century history as I, Mala Szorer, witnessed it.

I know that many people will wonder why I have suddenly decided to write this book. To them I would like to say that I have endured many sleepless nights. While floating between consciousness and semi-consciousness, I cry out, 'Dear Mother and Father! I am coming home to you at last. I want to see all of you once more in our cosy little house, with the river flowing so peacefully nearby, with white pebbles all along it, the ones that gave me hours of enjoyment when I was just a child. I long to see, once more, the green fields beyond our house where we relaxed and enjoyed long walks together. Please invite all my dear friends and put on a big feast, Mother dear, because I am coming to tell you the most horrendous story that you ever heard – about my miraculous circumvention of death on so many occasions and about my loneliness for so many years.'

A very familiar voice seems to be calling out as if from Heaven, 'Do not enter Tarnogród, my dear child. There is no one there to listen to you any more.' With a sudden quiver in my heart, I wake up from that fanciful vision, from that nightmare. When fully awake, I remember and soon determine to write my story – not just for my dear, lost, annihilated family and friends but for the whole world, so that they too may remember and not allow the memories of those dreadful happenings to fade away like leaves in autumn.

Tarnogród. As the immaculate boots of the Nazi soldiers trampled the pastoral tranquillity of that village in the Polish countryside, my life was about to change starkly and irrevocably. I was to be plucked from the warm bosom of my grandparents, parents, brother and sisters and cast out to survive as best as I could, to do battle with the elements in an increasingly hostile world.

Very soon events overtook my family and me, and the systematic annihilation of the Jewish population of Poland began. The appalling conditions that my people endured and the 'civilised' world's silence in the face of such evil stick in my mind like a yellowed, dog-eared photograph, the photograph of the most awful chapter in the history of mankind – the Holocaust. There is an old saying that 'others may fear what the morrow will bring, but I must tell the world what happened yesterday.' My story may seem fantastic or fanciful, but it is all true. It all happened to me in my lifetime, not a hundred years ago but just one short generation ago. We owe it to the dead to keep their memory alive by reminding the world of its responsibility never to forget. For to face the future one has to understand the past.

BOOK

F

BOOK ONE
Flight

1. The River Runs Peacefully

I was born into an observant Jewish family in Tarnogród, a small town deep in the heart of Poland in the vicinity of Lublin. My parents had nine children, three of whom died in infancy of dysentery and influenza, illnesses for which there was no cure in those days. In retrospect, I can see that they were the lucky ones, for they were spared the agonies and suffering that lay in store for the rest of my family.

In the early 1930s, my father, Yitzchak Szorer, left for Uruguay on a business venture. Times were very hard in Poland, and he was the only breadwinner in our family. His brothers Jacob and Meilich were already there, and they settled in Uruguay for good. Thus they escaped the events that were to bring about the annihilation of my entire family and of six million of our people.

About two years after his departure to South America, my father returned to Tarnogród, to my mother and us children, from whom he could not be parted any longer. At first he believed that he could settle in Uruguay, but he soon realised that it would be too difficult to bring up children there in a religious manner, for at that time Uruguay had no Jewish schools or even an established Jewish community.

To sustain our large family, my father engaged in many

small businesses, but eventually he gave those up and decided to become a wholesaler of fruit. He began by leasing a few orchards on the outskirts of our town. Later, he leased them from farmers in adjoining villages like Łukowa and Chmielek and other places whose names I no longer recall. He would lease the orchards when the trees were still in bloom, so that he could estimate how much fruit they would produce. He was very seldom wrong. Although we were never rich, we somehow managed to exist on the profits of those fruit, and we also had enough fruit for ourselves, which kept us all healthy.

'Thank Heaven that I did not stay in Uruguay,' my father used to say, 'for in Tarnogród we could become educated and still observe our religion to the full.'

While in Uruguay, my father was very successful in his business venture and he managed to save enough money to build a new house for us, adjoining that of my maternal grandfather, Reb Yaakov, or Yanchi as he was affectionately known to the townspeople.

Although my grandfather was an elderly man, he was still quite strong and active. He and his brother Issar were so robust that they were playfully nicknamed 'Cossacks'. The townsfolk joked that the two could carry a whole house on their shoulders. My grandfather was a *melamed* at the local *cheder*, and I learned a lot just by listening to his stories. He was a widower and, apart from the cooking that my mother did for him, he looked after himself and his house perfectly well. He always looked very neat and tidy. I can still remember the wooden planks he laid all around our houses, so we could visit him without getting mud on our shoes, especially in winter; for concrete was not yet available in those days.

Even without many extras, we considered ourselves luckier than some of our neighbours, because we possessed two particular luxuries which made us the envy of our acquaintances – an outdoor toilet and our own little well. We allowed our neighbours to share our water, which we used for cleaning and washing linen only. We had to walk a little way for drinking water, but sometimes we could afford to have it delivered to our house, and that made life slightly easier for us.

Ours was a simple home, like most others in our town, where many inhabitants were as poor as we were. A big oven in the centre of a large room divided my parents' bedroom from the dining room. That oven was used for baking and for keeping us warm during the cold winters. We also had a separate stove for cooking meals. Since there was no gas or electricity in our house, wood provided the only source of fuel. We got our supply of wood every Tuesday, which was market day in town. My father had a long-standing arrangement with a peasant who, for a fee, delivered tree trunks to our house in a horse-drawn cart.

The Nitka ('Thread') River ran near our house, and we used to rinse all our clothes in it as the well water was insufficient for all our needs. Miraculously, our laundry always came out sparkling clean. During the summer, we also used to wash our crockery, cooking utensils and cutlery in the small river, leaving them to dry in the sun on wooden crates. Since we never knew any luxuries, we grew accustomed to those conditions, for we knew our parents laboured hard to feed and clothe us. They tried to make sure that we were kept happy. It was customary in our home to always say our morning prayers before eating our breakfast. We also prayed before we went to sleep at night and we said our grace after eating. I enjoyed life to the full, never expecting more from it than my dear parents could afford to give, never forgetting to thank the Almighty for all we did possess.

My favourite pastime was playing with the pebbles that lined the bottom of the Nitka River, and I became quite an expert at it, throwing up four or five at a time and catching them all together. Beyond the river there were cornfields and orchards. I loved walking around the narrow grass pathways which surrounded those cornfields. Most of all, I loved lying beneath the trees and staring up at the beautiful blue sky. The trees were always my best friends. I would do my homework under them, and they instilled in me the creative inspiration I needed for writing poems in Polish or in Yiddish.

Every summer we left the unbearable heat to spend time in the orchards we leased. Every orchard had a little hut in the middle of it, and we would bring with us our cooking utensils, food, blankets and other essentials. How we all loved the food that Mother cooked on a small stove outside the hut. We children slept peacefully in the vast garden, although our parents had to keep a vigilant watch to make sure no one stole the ripe fruit. The fresh air gave us all a healthy appetite, so that at the end of the summer we returned home refreshed and in good spirits.

But as much as I enjoyed the outdoor life, I liked even more returning home to begin a new year of school, eager to move up to a new class and explore new subjects. I could never understand why some of my friends longed to stay away from school forever. They did not realise that once they left the school they could never return to it. Because there was no money to send me to a private Jewish school, I attended the state school. Nevertheless, I observed all the *mitzvos*. I even taught the non-Jewish girls to say a prayer over food.

Ours was a very close-knit community that shared its joyous occasions as well as its grief. When a member of the community got married, we all celebrated. We did not care that we always wore the same dresses as long as we enjoyed ourselves. We were all one big, happy family, and together we feasted on the joys of village life with all our friends. There was never a dull moment in my childhood.

2. Strange Lessons at School

Our good fortune was not to last forever. In 1936, severe hailstorms ruined all the crops in our part of the country and brought our relative prosperity to an abrupt end. Conditions were now very difficult for us, and there was not always enough money. Nevertheless, our parents cheered us up all the time, telling us to trust in Heaven. In the meantime, we had to make our clothes last for a long time.

With the worsening nationwide economic situation, the local crisis suddenly aroused ugly anti-Semitic passions, causing shockwaves to sweep through every Jewish community in Poland. Tarnogród was no exception. At the start, however, it did not make much difference to us children when the storms left us almost destitute. We children carried on living happily, for we were still too young to be concerned.

Although our town was small, there were two schools in it. The one I attended was called Zajacowka, a beautiful building beyond a river, surrounded by gardens and large playing fields. Occasionally, we went on outings to the nearby woodlands of Majdan. I loved these trips, for they took me away from my overcrowded home for a few hours into the leafy green expanses of my beloved countryside.

In the winter, I would ski to school, towing my sled along for the compulsory winter sports. After school, we played our own winter sports. We had plenty of time for our games, for the snow almost never melted until springtime. With the bright moon in the starlit blue-black sky and the sparkling white snow deep on the frozen soil, we would climb a different hill every evening and joyously slide down the other side with the crisp night air whistling past our ears. Invigorated, we would all return home with glowing cheeks and healthy appetites to the hot meals our mothers had prepared for us.

Everything looked so beautiful to me, and I believed that all people were our friends. Only later did I realise how wrong and naive I was.

Before long, we Jewish students began to feel unsafe on the way to school and on our return from school, and very soon, the schoolroom itself became dangerous for Jewish children.

It was customary for all of us to rise when a teacher entered the classroom and to sit down upon his command. One day, still half asleep, I was a second late in obeying the command to sit down. The teacher, a man named Smutek, suddenly came up to me and beat me so ferociously with a ruler that I blacked out. When I regained consciousness, I could not remember what had happened to me. During recess, my friends told me that Smutek had beaten me into unconsciousness because I did not sit down quickly enough. Little did my teacher understand that I was still tired and half asleep then, having shared a bed with one or two sisters. But I was hungry for knowledge, and I had to swallow the insults and physical abuse, even if it was insensitive.

One teacher named Herr Weiss, probably an ethnic German, would often threaten us with remarks like, 'Wait till the Germans come.' Since we did not understand what he meant, we did not tell our parents.

As much as I loved learning, soon even I began to feel uneasy about going to school. But I was always the tough one, and my parents used to say that I should have been born a boy as that would have suited them very well, because they only had one son, my elder brother by two years, Yechiel Gershon.

One day, Herr Weiss kept all the Jewish boys after class, my brother Yechiel among them, and he caned them all although they had not done anything wrong. When a delegation of distraught mothers went to his house to complain, he chased them away with derogatory remarks. School being compulsory, the boys had no choice but to continue attending classes.

I can still see the sad look on my mother's face as she said goodbye to her son every morning. We could not complain to the police, since we were afraid of them too. To this day, I smile politely at every police officer I see. They must wonder at my 'friendliness', for I have not shaken the belief that if we 'behave', and if we are 'grateful', the police would be our friends. At least, they would leave us alone.

3. A Varied Education

The police did not leave us alone. With each passing day, life became more and more difficult for the Jewish community, and anti-Semitic acts became increasingly commonplace.

Every morning, an old Jewish bagel seller would arrange his wares neatly on white paper napkins in a big wicker basket. He would then take the bagels to the town square and peddle them. How petrified I was when I saw a burly police officer step on the basket and trample the bagels with his dirty boots. He walked away without any sign of remorse; I could see that he even had a smile on his face. I was soon to witness many such traumatic incidents as the great tragedy unfolded. It soon became apparent to me that there were more bad people in the world than good ones, and I changed from a happy-go-lucky child to a serious one as I began to see things I could never have imagined. I must have matured in that one year the equivalent of a few, when I began to understand how difficult our situation had become, but I carried on as usual, for ours was a happy home where our parents' instructions were usually carried out to the full. When we were told not to worry, we pretended not to worry.

It did not take long before we were reduced to extreme

poverty, and we could not even afford to buy the much-needed eiderdowns. The winters in Poland were very harsh, and heating in our house was non-existent, except when my mother's cooking took the chill out of the air. My parents, as resourceful as ever, decided that we would make our own eiderdowns. We all sat round a big table and removed the fleece from the hard stems of duck and goose feathers. After several such sessions, which we all thoroughly enjoyed, we had plucked enough plumage to make an eiderdown. Although my mother was not a professional seamstress, she managed to make covers which we all helped stuff with the feathers. Once they were full, my mother sewed up the opening through which we had stuffed the down. This activity was repeated every time we needed another eiderdown. Our neighbours did the same in their homes, for there were very few rich people in the whole of our town.

My parents were very musical and would often join us in song during those sessions. Sometimes they told us to recite the poems that we knew by heart; we knew so many that we were never lonely or bored. Now our new eiderdowns added physical warmth and cosiness to the long and frosty Polish winter. The knowledge that we had made them all by ourselves gave us great satisfaction, and we enjoyed sleeping under them all the more. Next to food, they were the most essential items in the house.

Sometimes I would overhear my parents and their friends discussing world issues uneasily, but I was too young to understand or really care about these grown-up things. I then believed those were not really my concern. In my mind, the only worry my parents had was how to clothe and feed our large family.

My father's mother, Rivka, was a widow who remarried; her new husband was Moshe Brand, a kind gentleman. They lived in a faraway village called Pysznica, near Nisko. They seemed to be well-off, because every time my father visited them, he brought home a lot of cooked food and preserved meats. As a widow, my grandmother had been a cook in a Warsaw restaurant. She stopped working after she remarried, but she would make lovely dishes and bake beautiful cakes and have her friends deliver them to us. We were very hungry in those days although the war had not yet started.

Because I worked hard, even as a child, my appetite was always good. To this day, I remember having to write an essay at school on a favourite topic. I wrote about food, which made everyone laugh.

When my oldest sister Balla left school at the age of fourteen, as was then customary in Poland, my grandmother invited her to Pysznica and paid for her to learn top-class dressmaking. After completing her apprenticeship when she was eighteen, Balla started her own small, but successful, dressmaking business in Warsaw.

My parents used to tell me that after I finished school and my apprenticeship I would go to Warsaw to join my big sister. I was curious to see the big city, and I loved and admired Balla very much, but I had different ideas. I thought I was capable of more than dressmaking – if I only had the opportunity to study. I loved school more than anything else; every new subject fascinated me, and I always aimed to be at the top of my class. My parents were very pleased with me, and I used to get special treats like a big red apple, which I thoroughly enjoyed. They could not afford more costly treats.

Whenever a government inspector was expected at the school, I was told to sit at the front near the headmaster, Kierownik. Before the inspector arrived, I was given a new uniform for the day. My own uniform, although quite clean, was patched in places and a little faded from the numerous launderings it had withstood. It was the last uniform I wore, and it was grey with white edging on the pockets. The collar was white and had little embroidered flowers at each corner.

When the inspector arrived, he would test us on all the subjects, asking a variety of questions. I always answered them correctly, much to the delight of our headmaster. On other occasions, the headmaster hardly noticed me and did not even always answer my greeting. My faded uniform probably did not please his eye.

Outside the classroom, the teachers taught us to be industrious; there was no need for a janitor in our school as it was the duty of every pupil, in rotation, be it girl or boy, to sweep the floor and take care of the general tidiness of the building. As a result, we all became very 'house proud', and we loved our school as if it were our own home.

There were other lessons about the virtue of prudence. A big notice on the wall over the school's stationery shop declared: *SPÓŁDZIELNIA KREDYTU NIE UDZIELA!* CREDIT IS NOT ALLOWED HERE! Even at an early age, we learned the value of money and the self-discipline not to spend what we did not have – a lesson that has stood me in good stead throughout my life, especially throughout my childhood.

There were many trees in our neighbourhood, and near our house there grew one called *laska*. The bark peeled away easily, and we made our own counting sticks and whistles from its branches. In those days, there was no money for new toys.

Often during school holidays, I would walk two hours to a village called Łuchów Dolny to visit my uncle Abram, my mother's brother. He and his family shared a large house with his brother-in-law Shimon and his family. They were small-scale farmers and also had a small grocery shop. Although they lived together for many years and shared the dining room, they never quarrelled but lived in harmony with my aunt's old parents.

As young as I was, I admired their way of life. I enjoyed farm work, especially reaping corn with a sickle, as it was still done in those days, or digging up potatoes, at which I became expert.

My favourite agricultural pastime was looking after the cows, as I was then left alone and could sing all the songs I learned at school. I could not do that often in front of other people. I loved to sing, but others were not so appreciative of my musical talents. It was only on occasions such as these, when I was completely alone, that I could indulge myself. I also used these singing sessions to improve my Polish pronunciation. Poland had only been reunited since 1918, and because my parents had lived under Russian and Austro-Hungarian rule until their early twenties, their Polish was not fluent. I had no concept in those days of how vital the language would one day become in order to save my life.

4. Summer Turns to War

One evening in late August 1939, towards the end of my vacation on my uncle's farm, I went to bed early. Upon hearing voices outside, I woke up and went for a stroll around the farm. Looking up at the dark sky, I saw soldiers, holding large rifles, falling from the sky.

The following day, we learned that the German invasion of Poland had already begun, and I decided to go back home to be with my family. I did not fully understand what war meant. From my history lessons, I knew only that many soldiers die in wars. Never did I dream that so many millions of innocent people and their children would be slaughtered for no reason other than that they had a different religion or a different heritage.

The summer holiday had finally ended, and despite recent developments, I eagerly awaited the start of the new school year and my promotion to the next class. I also couldn't get home quickly enough to tell my parents that I had inherited my older cousin Eli's textbooks. That meant my parents would not have to spend any money for new ones. Until then, I had to borrow them from friends to do my homework. How I cherished those newly acquired precious books. I covered them with patterned paper and proudly wrote my name and 'Class 6' on every one of them.

On the first Friday evening after the vacation, my father returned home from *shul* with the news that the Germans had already occupied Lancut, a town about sixty miles from Tarnogród, the previous day.

Seeing how alarmed we looked, he soon calmed us by saying, 'Things can hardly get any worse than they already are.' He told us not to worry but to carry on as usual.

'Who knows? Maybe our lot will improve,' my mother remarked.

Without a radio or newspaper, my parents were quite ignorant of what was really happening in the world. Only rich people could afford a radio or newspaper in our town, and very few adults were fluent in the Polish language. My mother still wrote letters to her brother in Palestine in German.

The following day, we heard a lot of shooting as Polish soldiers bravely but forlornly tried to defend our town against the mighty German army. Unprepared and taken by surprise, many fell in battle. We all lay down on the floor every time there was a loud bang from one of the large German cannons. Before long, we heard that the powerful German army was about to march into Tarnogród.

We all, especially the children, lined up and stared admiringly at the shiny boots and pressed uniforms of the Nazi soldiers. One could see that they had not encountered a lot of opposition because they all looked fresh, with arrogant pride in their faces. First came the tanks, then the cavalry and, finally, the infantry.

'These are real soldiers,' some of my friends said. 'Not from picture books.'

The euphoria soon came to an end when we saw a small Jewish boy shot dead in cold blood. He had been running home to tell his parents what he had seen. Now we were afraid to run, and we left slowly and dejectedly. At home, we were all told to recite *Tehillim*, and we all now realised that this was a heartless army after all.

I began to wonder what the soldiers' aim was, not yet being able to perceive fully the seriousness of our situation or to make any judgements about other people's opinions. I tried to stop being philosophical and carried on with my duties, like helping my mother with the younger children.

Events soon took a turn for the worse and instilled great fear in all our hearts.

5. A Different Kind of Soldier

Not too far from our house lived a well-to-do Christian family who had a radio, which was a luxury in those days. Their daughter, who was a friend of mine, invited me to their house to listen to the news. What I heard made my blood boil. I was speechless and could not get up from my chair for quite a few minutes. Reporting on Hitler's propaganda broadcast, the commentator said that Hitler had promised to salute any Jew still left alive in 1944.

Lying in bed that night, I tried to visualise what this monster called Hitler looked like, for I could not imagine that he resembled any human being. I decided not to tell my family what I had heard on the news. For quite a while, I told no one. I do not think they would have believed me had I told them.

It did not take long before we were separated from the Christian people of the town. One day, we heard that there was a town crier – something we had never heard of until then. He went through town with a loud bell which brought all the inhabitants outdoors. He then announced that the Jewish children were no longer permitted to go back to school. Now it was my turn to cry, for I sensed that this was the beginning of a dreadful and uncertain future. At the time, this was my biggest worry.

I resolved to make the best use of the precious books that my cousin had given me. Every time I finished helping my mother clean the house or look after the younger children, I lay on the grass outside, reading aloud and teaching myself history, geography, Polish and nature studies, which I loved immensely. Arithmetic was the only subject I could not master without help. How I wished my oldest sister Balla could have been at home to help me. Little did I know that Warsaw had already been bombed and that Balla and many others like her were already on their way back to the small towns, where they believed life would be more peaceful. They were soon disappointed at how quickly the Germans managed to find and occupy even the smallest town or village.

Being as bored as I was, my Jewish school friends and I decided to form a school of our own. We read to each other and set ourselves daily lessons. We felt quite excited to be playing the role of schoolteachers. As a result of reading aloud a lot, my Polish pronunciation improved to such an extent that I sounded just like a non-Jewish Polish girl. I also looked like one. I had light blond hair, blue eyes and a fair complexion, unlike my sister Balla who had dark hair and brown eyes. My looks were to prove essential to my survival on many occasions in the years to come.

Although I was young in years, I soon matured enough to realise what lay ahead of us. I decided to put up a big fight. My mind and education were broadened by reading *Sabina*, serialised magazines Balla had sent me from

Warsaw. Her long letters describing life in the big city fascinated me. I found it hard to understand, for instance, that in Warsaw one did not always know one's immediate neighbours, since people minded their own business. In our small town of Tarnogród, everyone knew everything about everyone. As friendly as I was, I believed privacy was sometimes necessary. But this was non-existent in our town, and we lived as one large family.

I looked forward to the day when I would be able to see the big city for myself. In my mother's eyes, I was already a dressmaker. Did I not know how to make invisible repairs to torn garments? Did I not know how to make handbags from cardboard and pieces of material, and embroider them? Despite our poverty, my mother had a matching handbag for almost every dress, courtesy of my handiwork and the leftovers of material that Balla used to send home.

Soon, city life seemed like a dream which I would never attain, for our area of Tarnogród was changed to a ghetto. Whenever I became sad, I cheered myself up by thinking of *Hashem*, the only One in whom I had trust; I prayed, and all of a sudden, I would feel strong. I believed that I could fight all our enemies and win freedom for my family and all the oppressed people. I even secretly dreamed of invisibly breaking into the headquarters of the Gestapo and murdering all of them with a long stick with a hook at the end. Indeed, we possessed such a 'weapon': we used it to retrieve the water bucket from the bottom of the well when the cord snapped. However, I had to be content with my dream only.

In spite of being weakened by constant pangs of hunger, my father spent many an hour chopping the tree trunks into firewood. With the little money that he saved, we bought a pitiable amount of food. But this did not last very long, and within a short space of time, we were forced to sell off our bedspreads, most of the household utensils and lighting. We kept one tiny lamp, so we would not have to sit in complete darkness.

Our parents kept up our spirits by singing and playing games with us. We did not have any toys, but we had many homemade games, which cheered up the young children.

It did not take very long for my family, along with the rest of the Jewish community, to be reduced to starvation. I could not bear to see the misery around us, especially my three little sisters who were by now too weak to cry. Since I was also the most daring, I began thinking about ways to find food for my starving family. I looked for another girl to join me in my burdensome task but could not find any. I quickly decided I would have to carry out my surreptitious activities alone.

Soon, more trouble was on the way. One day, the town crier announced that every Jewish person – man, woman and even child – had to wear a yellow Star of David at all times. The star had to be sewn onto a white background so that it could be seen from afar. In line with our tormentors' disregard for human life and dignity, they decreed the death penalty for disobeying this order.

I used to observe the soldiers. I had never been to

Germany, and I began to wonder what their country looked like. Now, Poland was also theirs, and so were we. We became their possessions, and everything we had belonged to them. Though I am a peaceful person, many times I was so cross that I felt like fighting a soldier, taking his gun away and then shooting the whole lot of them.

In their arrogance, the Nazis now forbade the holding of services in our *shul* and also prohibited assembly of any kind by more than three people. Our *shul*, a beautiful eighteenth-century building perched on top of a hill, was soon converted into a stable for German cavalry horses. The smaller *Belzer Shtiebl* was transformed into a hospital for typhoid and other victims, for many epidemics were now raging. No one was allowed in to help those unfortunate people and, without medicine and without food, many died there every day. It is hard to understand why no member of my family picked up any of those diseases as we lived nearby. Perhaps the germs could not spread that far, not having had enough nourishment from the dying people.

In desperation, my fourteen-year-old brother Yechiel and I decided to leave the house to beg for food from farmers or soldiers in the surrounding villages. Not long before that, I had knitted a cardigan out of some unravelled sweaters for my seven-year-old sister Kresele. I took it with me and bartered it for a loaf of bread, a few potatoes and some eggs. Though I got good food for it, I was not happy that it would be worn by one of those beastly soldiers' children. To this day, whenever I see a cardigan knitted in a zig-zag pattern, especially if it is made out of red, white and blue wool, it sends a shiver of trepidation up my spine.

While out begging in the villages, we had also been treated to some bread and milk by some peasants, and we excitedly made our way back home with our newly acquired treasures. Although we were both very hungry, we resisted the urge to take even the smallest of bites out of the bread. We wanted to share our provisions with the rest of the family. I imagined the feast our mother would prepare and how Kresele would get an extra large portion for sacrificing her cardigan.

We were not far from Tarnogród now and believed that we were out of danger. I was imagining how our family would soon be hugging and kissing us and thanking us for the lovely food which we had brought home. Suddenly, we spotted two mounted SS officers dressed in their distinctive black uniforms. They also spotted us and began to shout in that all-too-familiar superior tone of voice, '*Halt!*'

Instinctively, we ran into a cornfield and obeyed their command. They, too, stopped, took aim and shot at us. I pretended to have been hit and fell with outstretched arms. I remained motionless on the ground for a few minutes, hoping that my brother had done the same. After the Nazi officers had ridden away, thinking that they had done a good job on both of us, I raised my head a little and froze when I realised that Yechiel would never get up again. He had been hit and killed outright, not even having had time to moan.

I lay down for a little while, not daring to pick myself up in case the beasts would return to investigate, but they did not. They must have believed this mission was completed and gone looking for others. I knew I had to take a big risk and attempt to go home; I could not stay in the cornfield indefinitely.

Now there was no time to shed any tears, for someone could have heard me and asked me what had happened. I was still a little way from Tarnogród, so I was not out of danger yet. I knew that my brother would never be hungry any more and he was, therefore, better off than the rest of us. But I also knew that my dear parents would think differently. They would have lost a child, their only son.

Secretly, I envied Yechiel and hated the task I now had to carry out, to tell my dear parents that their only son, the apple of their eye, was no more. Picking up my sack and placing it on my shoulder like the professional beggar I had now become, I made my way slowly back home. I did not meet any more Germans on the highway. Once I had entered the town, however, I saw many soldiers, but miraculously they took no notice of me. They all seemed to ignore me, as if I did not even exist. I touched myself to make sure that I was still alive and carried on walking, thanking *Hashem* for saving me. I did not know how much longer I would be that lucky.

When I arrived home, my feelings were still suppressed after witnessing the killing of my own brother in cold blood. I was still in shock and could not even cry; no tears came flowing out of my eyes, and I remained speechless for a long time. My parents didn't even need to question me, for they understood quite well what had happened. They went quietly to our grandfather's house to cry, so that my little sisters would not hear them.

We all mourned the death of our dear Yechiel privately. All except the three young ones, who were happy with the food I brought home. They were too young to understand what had happened and must have believed that Yechiel was still out begging for them.

Now we had another problem with which to contend. The town's younger water carrier was a simpleton who could not even remember how old he was. No one had taken any notice of him until the Germans appointed him to be their informer. For his services, they gave him a nice house to live in and a German uniform to wear. He had never felt so important. The cunning Nazis used his services to betray his own people and now instructed him to question anyone whose children were seen leaving the ghetto that day.

When I learned about the water carrier's new role, I knew what I had to do. I would have to become a soldier. I did not have a gun, but I was armed with a very strong will to survive. I would not surrender so easily, and this foolish man was not going to have a chance to betray me.

I managed to slip out of the back of our house, together with my cat. This cat and I had a long-standing relationship. Since I had been a small child, she had followed me all over and sat silently near me when I played with other children. My playmates had always teased me that the cat was winning all the games for me.

The cat and I were soon on the other side of the Nitka River, and we hurriedly left the big garden for the fields. I was free once more even if it was for a short time only. I felt hungry and began to eat the little bit of food I had dared to take from my family; I knew that without food my needed energy would soon disappear.

As we expected, the water carrier soon informed the Germans that Yechiel and I were the Szorers' children, and they forced my father to go and bury us. No one had gone to check the scene of the 'crime', and the Germans never found out that I had escaped. From then on, it was not safe for me to live at home. The only time I would go there would be to bring food for my now desperate, starving family. I decided that I would be safer without the Star of David and began removing it before going home; I kept it in my pocket, ready to put it on if I saw any Germans. This would not have helped me, since I was not allowed to leave the ghetto. Had I been spotted, they certainly would have shot me.

I also had to come home and report to work in place of Balla, who had returned from Warsaw. My name was called out as 'Balla' instead of 'Mala', and the others did not betray me. Balla stayed at home, for I was considered to be much stronger and more able to bear the pain, hunger and loneliness in the outside world. I knew that I was safer in the fields than with my family. Whenever I prayed, I became hopeful. I trusted in *Hashem* to make my prayers come true, like a baby trusts its mother.

I was so lonely that I began to think that the cat, with its soft eyes, looked at me as if she understood my suffering. I nicknamed her Malach, which means 'angel' in Hebrew, and I imagined that she was a real angel watching over me. I was not worthy of a real one, that much I knew. I was, nevertheless, glad she followed me around. How sorry I was that I had no food for her. I was afraid she would not survive, but she seemed to thrive without my help.

Although I secretly entered my parents' house on many occasions, I was not allowed to bring the cat in with me. However, the cat was always there when I left the ghetto, unnoticed even by the neighbours. Little did I know at the time how that cat was to play such an important part in my life.

Fortunately, I always managed to find food and bring it home without anyone seeing me enter the town. Only my cat was a witness.

6. My Guardian Was an Angel

During the severe winter of 1940, the Germans ordered children, some as young as eight years old, to clear the roads with shovels as the snow was very deep and the roads were impassable to cars. Some of the children were hardly as tall as the shovels they wielded. I was almost fourteen years old and tough enough to cope with frozen fingers and toes, as well as the hunger, to which I became accustomed. But many of the younger children perished in the snow, unable to withstand the merciless, inhumane conditions, and their poor parents were unable to help them.

On one occasion, when I went to work as Balla, our group of girls was taken to the Gestapo headquarters, housed in the priest's beautiful residence. The estate was surrounded by tall trees, a frozen garden and flower beds. We were asked to wash cars with freezing water in sub-zero temperatures. Soon, our fingers became frozen too, and we slowed down. The soldier supervising the car-washing began hitting us with a truncheon, telling us to work faster. I thought enviously of my brother Yechiel who had it all behind him. I decided that I had had enough too, and I was determined to take a big risk, knowing quite well what the consequences would be. I felt sorry for my dear parents who were going to lose another child. But enough was enough. My hands were numb, and I was not going to wash Gestapo cars any more. I was now ready to die. I was not afraid, or at least, I pretended not to be. I could not understand myself or what prompted me to behave in that manner, but my mind was fully made up. No more suffering for me.

I gave my beloved cat a big smile and said a fond goodbye to her. Then, I went up to the soldier.

'Either you stop hitting us, or I will stop washing the car,' I said to him.

'What did you say?' he asked. 'Did I hear right? Come with me.'

I followed him to a room where a high-ranking officer sat. When he saw me, he told the soldier to leave me to him and to go back to the others.

I wondered if he was going to shoot me in that elegant room of his, but he kept on writing. I looked on, waiting for him to take down the big shotgun hanging on the wall and hoping that I would soon not feel the cold and hunger any longer. I was surprised to see that he did not even glance at his gun. How was he going to kill me? If he was going to use his bare hands, I was going to hurt him before I died. Or maybe I should kill him first? No! Then my whole family would be mercilessly tortured before being killed. Better that I should die than all the others. But who would then beg for food? I decided that without my help, they would not last very long, and we would all be reunited.

I took another look at the officer. I was relieved to observe that, unlike the soldier who brought me to him, he had a very friendly face. But he was the head of the Gestapo, I reminded myself, and heavily decorated. He began to speak to me now.

'Wash your hands and make my bed,' he instructed.

I carried out his command very carefully and made sure that the linen remained as clean as it looked when I first saw it.

'Now clean my boots,' he told me when I finished making his bed.

I polished those high boots which were worn by all Gestapo men. I enjoyed the respite from the arctic conditions outside, though I knew it was only temporary.

'Now wash the floor,' he said, in a most civilised manner.

While I worked, he continued writing, but I could see he was observing me all the time. I could not believe my eyes when, all of a sudden, I saw tears pouring down his cheeks. I, too, began to cry. He must be feeling sorry for me, I said to myself, because now he has to shoot me, and it does not look as if he is going to enjoy it.

'Is this your cat?' he said, indicating Malach who was watching me, having slipped in unnoticed.

'Yes, it is,' I said. 'My own angel, I believe.'

'Now promise not to tell anyone what I am going to do,' he said. 'I am going to send you home through the back door, and here is something for you.'

He gave me a large loaf of bread and a packet of sweets and instructed me not to tell anyone that he had given them to me, should I be seen on the way. Somewhat dazed by the turn of events, I ran home happily with my treasures, not understanding why I had merited such good treatment.

'My guardian is an angel,' I said to myself along the way. 'Otherwise, this would not have happened to me.'

When I told my father about my good fortune, he said, 'That was no ordinary man but an angel sitting temporarily in the Gestapo office.'

I joined in with my family, and together we had some bread and some sweets. The rest was put away for later. Everyone kissed me and said, 'What would we do without you?' I was pleased my plan had not worked.

There was no time to relax, and I played havoc with my brain about what to do next. I took out my *Tehillim*, and I began to pray. I wished I could take that *Tehillim* with me, but I knew it would put my life in jeopardy. After saying a few *kapitlach Tehillim*, I felt stronger than before. It was as if someone else's strength entered my body, and with it grew my determination to survive.

My parents did not protest when, time and again, I removed my yellow Star of David and left the ghetto with my cat by my side. Winter or no winter, the ghetto was not for me. The situation had become so desperate that even water had become difficult to obtain. People took a great risk to go a little way to the well and bring home a bucket of precious water.

Now I had to choose between being shot or dying of starvation, which was a much slower death. Indefatigably, I continued visiting the many small villages around our town, desperately begging for food for my hungry family. I assured my parents that I was not in the least bit afraid, and they believed me, having no alternative. None of us dared show any emotion, knowing very well the hopelessness of the situation. We all understood that it was only a matter of time before we would all be dead.

Some older girls in our town managed to obtain fake birth certificates, my older sister Balla among them. As for me, I was not old enough for an identity card, but as it turned out, the false papers were useless anyway. They were just a means for the Poles to extort money and possessions from doomed victims.

7. A Dark Plan

When I heard that Balla had become engaged to a boy in Warsaw, I was flabbergasted. How could they bring children into this rotten world? I thought. But they were never given the opportunity anyway. Shortly afterwards, her fiancé was shot while trying to leave the ghetto in search of food for his family. From then on, Balla lost her will to live. She never left the house unless she was called by the Germans to help peel potatoes or to clean their soldiers' rooms.

The population of our ghetto swelled daily as we were joined by Jews who had been driven out of places like Lodz and Kalisz. Our little house became home to twenty-five or thirty such destitute people. Though they all knew they were doomed, they sang songs to their little children like *Mir Velen Zei Iberleben* (We Shall Outlive Them). The children believed their parents because they knew no better, and I was pleased to see the young ones smile for their sorrowful parents. How glad I was that I was not yet old enough to be a mother, for I would not have been able to convince my children about the future.

In the beginning of 1942, a curfew was imposed on the Jewish community from six o'clock in the evening until eight the following morning. Anyone who ventured out between those times was to be shot on sight. It was then that my sister Balla whispered to me that we should put on our *Shabbos* dresses and walk over the bridge to Mr Guziek's garden.

Mr Guziek had returned from South America some years earlier and built himself a beautiful villa on the other side of the Nitka River. In better times, he was a good friend of our father and loved to converse with him in Spanish. He was a tall, friendly man who was well-disposed toward the Jews. Soon after the invasion, Mr Guziek was forced to move into a house that had been requisitioned from a Jew. His own house was occupied by a high-ranking German officer, to whom we now planned to pay a visit.

'We'll go into Guziek's garden,' Balla informed me. 'Then, when the German sees us, he's bound to shoot at us because it's after six o'clock already.'

I knew she was right, that we would not survive the night, and it suddenly seemed pointless to carry on struggling against our inevitable fate. We were doomed to extinction, and delivery into that fate seemed like liberation. It would be good, I thought, not to have to make any more decisions, not to struggle and run, not to live with death always at my back.

Balla and I dressed quickly and, with tears in our eyes, embraced our parents for what we thought was to be the last time. They were so weak by now that they did not understand what we were going to do and did not even try to stop us. We left the house and started off in the direction of the Nitka River. All around us was quiet, except for the almost imperceptible patter of Malach who accompanied us on our sad journey.

I looked down at my cat and wondered if she was also going to be killed.

'You won't die,' I said to Malach. 'You're an unusual cat. Only we shall be killed.'

On the way there, I suddenly had pangs of conscience when I reminded myself that I was the only one who was capable of obtaining food for the rest of the family. How would they survive without me? I wondered. The thought also crossed my mind that after the Germans shot us they would discover where we lived and kill the rest of my family, as was their usual custom.

I told Balla about my misgivings, but she only said, 'It's too late to turn back now, Mala dear.'

We approached the destined house and saw a fat Nazi sitting in the garden enjoying the fresh air. He was eating a juicy, rosy apple on a nice plate. We were only a few feet away from him now, and we continued talking to each other in normal voices. But he did not seem to hear us. We started humming, but he didn't even glance in our direction. He merely finished his snack and went back into the house.

Feeling a mixture of disappointment and relief, we returned home, passing close by German soldiers with guns. Somehow, they all ignored us. As we re-entered the house, our parents hardly commented on our return at such a dangerous hour. Thus, our failed mission remained a secret from the rest of the family.

I felt restless and claustrophobic in the stuffy house and went to stand near an open window. I stared out at the deserted ghetto and suddenly observed a soldier with a rifle over his shoulder at the foot of the hill. This was a common sight. Soldiers roamed the ghetto at curfew eagerly, ready to 'carry out their duty', ready to shoot anyone who ventured out at night.

This soldier appeared bored and looked in every direction. He started up the hill to Różaniecka Street and stopped abruptly. I wondered if I should stop staring out of the window, but he was not looking in my direction. Something had caught his attention, and I became concerned about what he might do next. I wondered what he had spotted when he looked up at a neighbour's house. He was gazing up so intently.

Though I became quite frightened, I kept my eyes on him. Soon, I found out what interested him. In that house opposite ours lived a family with beautiful daughters, one of whom was looking out of a window. The soldier began talking to her and paying her compliments. She became frightened, probably thinking that he would ask her to step outside. She would have to obey his command. Then, once she was outside, he would shoot her. She was not allowed to be out, beautiful or not.

For a while, she ignored his compliments. But then she foolishly believed that it was wise to pay him some compliments, too.

She summoned up some courage and called out to him, 'You look like such a nice boy. I don't believe that you are capable of committing those dreadful crimes that your friends are committing against us.'

Instantly, the soldier underwent a complete metamorphosis. By telling him that he was more merciful than his friends, she had greatly offended him. He began calling this beautiful and gentle girl derogatory names. He took his rifle off his shoulder and shouted, 'You don't believe I could do such things? I had the same education as all my friends, and I was a very good scholar. Who do you think I am? Just watch me, you silly Jew. You'll soon find out.'

I watched in horror as he took his rifle off his shoulder and while shouting at her and calling her the most degrading names, he took aim at her little sister standing next to her. 'You silly Jewess,' he said again and again. I could see that his face became as red as a beetroot. No one else had ever underestimated his strength until this Jewish girl in front of him dared to do so. He was going to show her what he was capable of doing, and he therefore did not aim his gun at her.

I heard cries coming from the house and did not look out of the window any more that evening. There was nothing I could do. I wanted to pitch something heavy at his head, but I knew what the consequences would be.

I rested in a chair all night, reciting *Tehillim*, unable to sleep. I kept seeing that executioner in front of my eyes as if he were now quite near me. But I was glad to be alive, and that night I made up my mind never to surrender. I would not waste any time but go out once more and beg. It was a low profession, but I would learn to enjoy it, for I loved bringing food to my family. That would become my biggest pleasure.

I would continue living in the forest. I would continue visiting villages in the guise of a Christian girl. I would offer to help grind grain in exchange for a loaf of bread. I would teach little children to read for some milk or some cheese. I would do anything I could to keep myself and my family from starvation. And on *Shabbos*, I would return to the forest and rest. I suddenly remembered how young I was and I reminded myself that every birthday friends wished me to live until one hundred and twenty years. That was still a long time away and I had a lot to accomplish.

I left the ghetto the next morning and went to 'work' in a neighbouring village. I never found out if my little neighbour was killed outright or only wounded. My blood boiled as I thought of that poor girl. I felt as if my own sister had been shot, and I prayed that the soldier's day of reckoning would come soon.

'Did you see what I saw?' I asked Malach, not expecting a reply, of course.

I felt a little easier after uttering those words, and I began to stroke her fur and that calmed me down a little.

'Please promise me faithfully that you will never leave me,' I said to my silent friend. I tried to imagine that what I had witnessed was just a bad dream but soon remembered that it was not. I went begging for a warm milky soup, which I got from a kind peasant's wife. I did some repairs for her. Then I went into the forest, my temporary home which was then like paradise to me, except that all those lovely fruit trees were missing. Had they been growing there, there would have been no need for me to leave the forest.

8. A Young Provider

As the days passed, I became stronger and more and more determined to survive. I kept on eating everything I could, and I became fatter and fatter. My meals consisted mainly of milk, cream and white cottage cheese, as well as boiled eggs, when I was lucky.

How I wished I could have shared this food with my beloved family, but I had to consume these meals at the peasants' tables, who had no idea I had a family.

On one of my begging trips, I went to Łuchów Dolny to visit my Uncle Abram. Not only were he and his family living together with my aunt's sister Gitel and her husband Shimon, their children and parents, they were also forced to share their house with a wealthy Polish farmer from Poznan and his family. Their land had been confiscated and given to a member of the Volksdeutche, ethnic Germans who lived in Poland.

This family from Poznan, who seemed to be refined people, were very upset at having to leave their big farm and beautiful house to move into a crowded farmhouse with strangers. Had he wished, the Polish farmer could have turned my uncle and his family out of the house, but he took pity on them and let them stay. He allowed my Auntie Goldie to run the household and do the cooking, which was extremely polite of him.

While I was there, two SS men, a German and a Pole, came into the house and demanded a meal. My aunt began preparing the food with the few provisions she had saved in order to feed the members of the household.

As she worked, the German suddenly announced that he couldn't eat before killing a Jew and that he always killed one before eating or else the food did not taste good. Selecting my uncle as the victim, he ordered him outside and told him to stand with his face to the wall.

At that point, I was more enraged than afraid, and one thought kept repeating itself over and over: To what level had Hitler reduced his nation?

The Germans were below animals, who only kill when hungry. This beast had a good meal prepared for him – by my aunt who had used her last fresh eggs and bread. Addressing him silently, I asked, 'How can you kill someone whose wife has just prepared a delicious meal for you to swill, you pig?'

I could not visualise that German as having a heart. If only I could open his chest and look inside to see for myself. I felt strong enough to kill them both with some stones that were lying close by, but I knew what the consequences would be. Other Germans would come out to the farm and kill the whole family or perhaps even hundreds of others. I always cared for others more than for myself. I learned this from my dear parents. I almost volunteered to change places with my dear uncle, but I was afraid he would shoot us both. I was about to witness another murder in cold blood – and right in front of me this time.

We all stood there, too frightened to move. As my uncle stood against the wall, I could see his shoulders tremble slightly as he quietly awaited his fate. My aunt stayed in the kitchen, silently waiting for the pistol shot that was about to kill her dear husband. The Nazi slowly raised his gun and aimed it at my uncle's back. Then, all of a sudden, he lowered his arm and replaced his gun in its shiny leather holster and walked back into the house to eat his meal. When my uncle realised that he had been granted a reprieve, he almost collapsed with relief but quickly returned to the house to help my aunt with the meal. Why the SS man did not carry out his threat I will never know. We all felt great relief but knew how serious the situation had become.

I hope those two and many other heartless people like them were killed on the Russian front. How I wished I could carry out these killings myself. If only I had the strength of Samson, I thought. I soon reminded myself that I was not worthy of it or *Hashem* would have given it to me. Did I perhaps become too proud of myself and imagine I was better than the others? I began to ask *Hashem* for forgiveness, for my modesty had temporarily left me.

After they had filled their bellies, the two Gestapo men left. I watched as they mounted their horses and sat erect, with pride in their eyes. They looked immaculate in their black uniforms with their shiny golden buttons.

I wanted to write down what had happened, but I knew quite well what they would do to me if they found a diary on me. Anyway, I had no paper or pencil. Fortunately, I was blessed with a good memory.

'You are lucky you are not a human being,' I said to Malach. 'At least, you don't understand what we have to endure.'

The sun was shining brightly, and I looked out at the green fields with their ripening oats. Will we ever eat bread from those fields again? I wondered. I recalled a poem that my sister Balla composed called *Broit* (Bread):

> My father once came home in haste
> With a big smile upon his face.
> 'An important guest I've brought you see
> A loaf of bread I have with me.
> Please share it out and do not waste
> A little crumb from its face.
> For seldom is a guest so sweet
> That someone left there in the street
> Now it is all yours and also mine
> May Heaven preserve it for a very long time
> For it is not always that we can see
> Such a big treasure at our feet.'

As I gazed at the beauty of the countryside, a small bird flew down and stood close by on the ground. Then a pigeon joined it. I looked at them, envious of their freedom. If only I could send a message with those birds to a faraway land so that people would come to rescue us. I still tried to believe that it was all a bad dream. I would soon wake up from it, and the first steps I would make would be towards my dear home. I felt great guilt at being free while the others were locked up.

I soon reminded myself that I had a job to do. I left

Łuchów Dolny and headed back for Tarnogród. I had to help my family who were awaiting my return with the food that I had managed to collect.

Łuchów Dolny was a few hours' walk from my town, and I decided that if I saw a German I would hide in one of the cornfields along the way. After walking for a while, I sat down by the wayside to rest. I reminded myself about what the Gestapo man had wanted to do to my uncle, but strangely enough, I was not afraid. I thought I must have grown a few inches to feel so strong, but when I looked, I was surprised to see that I was still short.

I began to feel both hungry and thirsty, but I didn't allow myself the luxury of eating from the food I was taking back to Tarnogród to my beloved parents and sisters. I knew that my family was eagerly anticipating my return. I had become the most important member of the household.

I didn't enjoy my grown-up role. How I wished that my dear father could once again care for us and feed us. I would escape the horrors that had been thrust upon me, and escape back into the sunshine of my carefree childhood when the world was a beautiful place filled with kind people like my family. I would have liked nothing better than to revert to the days of playing and learning. How I longed to go back to school, to listen to the teacher talk about worlds we had never seen. I even longed to be able to work again, even harder than before, but in freedom. Was this too much to expect?

I began to regret ever having been naughty or

complaining. Had I not had everything I needed, food to eat and a bed in which to sleep? So what if my shoes had holes in them and my toes sometimes went numb in winter on the way to school? Were there not other children in the same situation? Did it really matter that I had to wear the same dress for a long time? How sorry I was now to have complained to my parents. I had had something more than material possessions — I had had the freedom to go out and play with my friends without fear. I longed for a life without any restriction. I decided that if I ever got that freedom back, I would then know how to appreciate it more. I would never again take all those things for granted. What a lovely childhood I have had, I suddenly remembered.

I made my way home and was dismayed to see that my family was so weak from hunger that they hardly had the strength to stand up. For days now, they had spent all their time resting to conserve their energy for emergencies.

The younger children slept more now than they did as newborn babies. They did not understand what was happening, and I helped to calm them with songs, which they seemed to enjoy in the absence of food. They believed me when I told them that conditions would soon improve. I promised to buy them new dresses and a lot of toys. I also promised to take them to Warsaw, to that big city, to see a train I had never seen yet.

Fortunately, not one member of the family had caught any of the diseases that were sweeping through the ghetto. Many of our neighbours had died, only to be replaced by newcomers from other towns. My grandmother Rivka had become ill, and she begged me for some hot soup because she could not swallow the hard pieces of bread that I brought home. But there was nothing with which to make soup, and she passed away. I helped my father put her in a box and together we buried her. I remember how pitifully small and light she had become.

I kept on with this pattern of entering and leaving the ghetto. My family became so accustomed to me sneaking out that they forgot the risks I took and the bullet that might have been waiting for me. I was glad they felt this way. After a while, I got used to discarding my yellow Star of David before leaving our little house. I got used to walking along the dark, country lanes between Tarnogród and the surrounding villages to beg for a few life-sustaining crumbs of bread. Sometimes, I got potatoes and even some eggs and milk. Then, I returned home with my precious cargo, and everybody hugged and kissed me and praised me for my cleverness. But every time I came home safely, I knew that I had help from above and that I was not cleverer than everyone else. I believed (and still believe) that I was kept alive to feed the others and that they were the worthy ones, not I. Not once did I forget to say my thank you prayers to *Hashem*.

9. Ransoming the Men

I had been in the forest for several days, suffering from hunger, for my begging trips had not been successful. I slept for long periods, dreaming about killing Nazis, day-dreaming about sharing hearty meals with my family, always awakening to the hopelessness of my reality. I became lonely and longed to see my parents and Balla. I needed to go home and play games with my little sisters and tell them stories about the many dogs I met and how none barked at me. I knew that if I stayed in the ghetto for any length of time, I might not be able to leave, but I decided, come what may, to spend a few days with my family.

As I walked into the ghetto, I saw my father enter the stable. When the troubles first started, my father had built a false wall there behind which he was able to hide for a time. But a soldier had also seen him entering the stable and followed him inside. I could hear him shouting at my father to come out. When my father emerged, the soldier was about to take him away to work from which many men did not return.

In desperation, I ran to the stable and jumped between them. I looked the soldier straight in the eye. 'I know that none of us will survive, and I, too, will not be here for long,' I said. 'But one day, retribution will come, and your daughter will have to beg for your life, like I have to beg for my father's now.'

He must have had a daughter of his own, because he left without looking at me, leaving my father behind. He must also have possessed a heart, and I could see that this soldier did not enjoy carrying out his instructions as much as his friends did. Perhaps this one and others like him were simply poor students who had not learned their lessons. After all, are there not good scholars and bad ones? Sadly, most had learned their lessons quite well.

During the days I was in the ghetto, the Nazis began desecrating the Jewish cemetery. They commanded the adult male Jews to remove the tombstones and break them into small pieces. They then forced the Jewish men to repave the road to Różaniec, a village about three miles away, with pieces of tombstones. As the men worked, their guards continually beat them with rifle butts and sticks.

Not long afterwards, they started rounding up even younger girls for slave labour as well. I still went to work in place of Balla, but luckily, my group's task was to clean the soldiers' rooms and to peel potatoes. When we had a nice supervisor, he allowed us to take the peels home after we completed our assignment. When the peels were available, I would gather some dry wood, and my mother would make a hot soup. The potato peels were a boon, for the Germans granted us only ten grams of bread a day. We had to stand in line for hours, and on several occasions I saw weak and old people collapse and die in front of me when the wait became too long.

49

The Germans, looking for an easy way to take all the valuables from us, rounded up quite a few men one day. They took them to the barracks at Bełżec. No one expected to see them alive again. To everyone's surprise, a few days later, the Germans invited the wives of the detained men to ransom their husbands with jewellery and other valuables that they had managed to hide away. In desperation, the wives accepted the offer in the hope of redeeming their loved ones. But after handing over their possessions, they found that many of the men were too weak to walk home. They bore the scars of floggings and beatings and had to be left to their fate. This practice was repeated many times. There was no transport for them, of course.

Girls were called to work one day, and I again went instead of Balla, who was too weak to stand now. A young Ukrainian was in charge of a group of half-starved girls, most of whom were about eighteen years of age. That Ukrainian was dressed in a very fine suit and strutted around pompously with pride in his eyes. The suit must have been removed from a Jewish boy he had killed. It was obvious that he enjoyed his job immensely, beating every one of us with great pleasure.

He made us lug heavy planks from one place to another and then back again. It did not take very long before we became too weak to carry on, and we tried to rest for a while. 'If you don't work harder,' said our tormentor viciously, 'I will push you even harder.' The girls did not move. They were too tired and resigned to their fate.

Looking around me at my workmates, I realised that I

had to do something. Summoning my last reserves of strength, I stood up and slowly walked over to the Ukrainian.

'Please be nice to us,' I implored. 'You have such a handsome face. Losing your temper all the time will only make that lovely skin of yours begin to wrinkle, which would be a great pity.'

It was only because I was so young that I dared to lie like that. He was really ugly with many spots on his face. For a minute, he looked at me as if he hadn't quite understood what I had said. Then he smiled and replied, 'This I like, and coming from such a young girl. You can have a break now, and I will allow you to go home soon. As for the rest of you, there will be no mercy from me.'

My ploy had not produced the desired result. I had really hoped to save all the others too, but there was nothing I could do for those unfortunate girls now. By the time I went home, they were so tired that they were moving even more slowly. I never found out when they were allowed to go home, for I never saw them again though I went to work many times.

Mostly, Ukrainians supervised our useless work. We had to carry those planks backwards and forwards to give the beastly supervisors satisfaction and to make them feel very important.

One freezing *Shabbos* morning, we were all ordered to leave our houses open and assemble in the Rynek marketplace. We took some personal belongings with us, but we dropped everything in a big pile when we saw that we were surrounded by SS troops with machine guns. We said the *Vidui*, our final prayers, and thought our last moments had come. But after the Germans selected about a hundred men and marched them off to the *shul* for detention, the rest of us were allowed to leave for home. My father was not detained, because the Germans had given him a work permit and made use of his skills. As we shuffled back in the direction of the ghetto, we heard the sound of automatic gunfire mixed with deafening screams coming from the *shul*. The soldiers had let off a few rounds of bullets in the air in order to frighten the women into giving up their remaining items of jewellery in exchange for the men's release.

Not long after the incident in the marketplace, soldiers came around the ghetto to demand all our jewellery and promised to free the men. Most of our jewellery had previously been collected to try to save the people of Bełżec, and we now had nothing much to give. We all parted with our valuables, like wedding rings and earrings. They must have got enough to satisfy them, for they freed those people immediately.

The Nazis tried to keep us isolated and cut off from other Jewish communities, but we knew that they usually collected their victims' valuables prior to carrying out extermination orders. They used the same tactics in every town to make sure that no one hid jewellery. None of the people had any illusions about their fate, but I still had hopes of surviving; I felt very much alive, and my will to live was great.

BOOK TWO
Shelter in the Forest

10. Goodbye, Family; Goodbye, Childhood

Early in the morning of *Erev Rosh Hashanah*, 1942, my father was saying *Selichos* – the prayers of repentance which are recited daily during the weeks leading up to *Yom Kippur*, the holiest day on the Jewish calendar. I was preparing to sneak out of the house in order to beg for food to sustain us over the High Holy Days. I hoped that my mother would not notice me leaving, as I tried to avoid a tearful farewell scene. But she called to me with tears in her eyes, saying, 'Go my daughter, go, and may *Hashem* help and protect you.' It was as if she sensed the impending calamity that was finally to befall us and part us from each other forever.

She would not have allowed me to venture out on such a day, when it was not certain that I would be able to return before sundown. But we needed food for two days, and we needed time to cook it before *Yom Tov*. I was determined to be home before sunset, and I secretly asked *Hashem* to help me in my difficult task. It was not raining, and that suited me well. I was also quite hungry.

With a very heavy heart, I embraced each one of my family and asked them not to worry about me. I did not then realise that they would never need my provisions again, that these were the last few hours of their lives.

I left the town, with Malach at my side as usual, and I passed many soldiers on the way. As usual, none of them paid any attention to me whatsoever, and I continued walking. When I was some distance away, I noticed troops encircling Tarnogród. I had no idea what they were planning to do. Reluctantly, I continued towards Korchów, a village I had visited several times before.

I was quite successful that day. I managed to get a fair number of potatoes, some pieces of bread and eggs. I had so much food that I afforded myself the luxury of tasting some of it, thus gaining strength which I would soon need. With the heavy sack on my shoulder, Malach and I set out on the journey back to Tarnogród, hoping to get home in time for my mother to prepare a cooked meal for us before *Rosh Hashanah* started.

From afar, I could see a figure walking toward me, coming nearer and nearer. Soon I recognised Mr Guziek, our nice Christian neighbour. When he came near me, he quietly told me that my parents and my sisters, along with many other young people, had been rounded up and taken to the marketplace. They had been informed that they would go to a much better place where the men would get good jobs, and their families would receive larger rations.

My parents had given my personal belongings to Mr Guziek to pass on to me before I joined them. He handed me a hot drink from a flask, and I drank some. It greatly refreshed me. He also had a note for me from Balla, which he said was important for me to read. I was too stunned and had to put the note away in my pocket, unable to read it in that state of shock. I collected my belongings from Mr Guziek's house and thanked him for his kindness, telling him that I fully realised that he had risked his life in meeting me. We met people on the way who believed I was his daughter.

Then I made my way back home. The house was now empty except for my old grandfather who was too weak to walk and had been left behind. The Nazis knew that without help he would soon starve and die. He was very confused and had no idea of what really happened. He wanted to know when everyone would be back. I gave him some food and told him that I was going to find out and come back to look after him. Being too old and too weak by now to comprehend the situation, he allowed my words to allay his fears and gave me his blessing as usual.

I left my bundle of clothes at home and went to the marketplace. I could see that there was a huge pile of personal belongings in the middle of the street. Cautiously, I approached and noticed my sister Balla intimating to me that I shouldn't come any nearer. She was clever and must have realised the end was near.

I struggled with my conscience, thinking I should throw in my lot with my family, knowing quite well that I would never see my loved ones again. But I could not make myself join the group.

With powerful feelings of guilt overwhelming me, I turned around and ran home to read the note Balla had left with Mr Guziek. I was afraid to read it outside in case someone saw me. I quickly entered the house and looked around. Everything was surprisingly tidy. My family must have believed that they would return. Then I read Balla's letter.

Dearest Mala,

We do not know what the future holds for us, but whatever it is, Mummy and Daddy pray for a better fate for you. The Germans say they will take us to a place called Izbice, where they say Daddy will have work, and we will get double rations. Although I wish you were with us, I have a premonition that it is best for you not to join us. You are strong and clever and will have a better chance of survival on your own. For in spite of the Germans' promises, we know we are doomed. Look after Grandfather for us and, as a last resort, try to go to Łuchów Dolny to stay with Uncle Abram and Auntie Goldie. Be brave and may Hashem *bless you. Remember, we all love you.*

Balla

'I love you, too,' I said aloud. There was no one near to hear me except my cat.

I felt desolate and completely forlorn. Disbelief engulfed my whole body. I closed my eyes and imagined that I too was among my dear ones. I stood motionless for quite a while and began to pray. 'Please, *Hashem*, don't let them suffer too much.'

I stayed in the house for a few days, unable to muster up the energy to move. One day, glancing quickly out of the window, I saw that the street was deserted. Those Jews who remained behind in the ghetto were so stunned by the round-up and quite afraid to venture outside.

I felt a great sense of duty towards my grandfather, but I was sure to be arrested if I stayed with him much longer. I was a 'wanted person', after all. Wanted for what? I wondered. I knew I had not committed any crimes for which I deserved to be arrested. It was those German barbarians who were guilty of the most heinous crimes possible and I secretly devised a plan as to how I would punish them if I were the judge but soon realised how foolish I was. There was a bigger Judge, and I had to leave it to Him, I decided.

I prepared some food for my grandfather and kissed him goodbye. I knew in my heart it would be a long time before I would see him again – perhaps forever.

'I will be back very soon, *Zeidy* dear,' I said to him. 'Please do not worry about me as I am quite capable of looking after myself.'

I was sure that soon other people would occupy our house and would help him. I hated having to forsake my grandfather, but I was now powerless to help him, as it was too dangerous for me to be with other Jews.

With that thought, I suddenly stopped feeling like a child. If I were to survive, I would have to behave like a grown-up and fend for myself. Turning to my cat, I said, 'Come along, it's time to leave,' and I set off with a small bundle over one shoulder, destination as yet undecided. 'I have plenty of time to think about that,' I said to myself. 'The only obligation I now have is to find a way of surviving in the big, wide world that *Hashem* created for all of us, not just for the Germans.'

There being no choice, I decided to live in the fields

forever. 'If you can do it,' I said to Malach, 'then so can I. And from now on, I am going to compete with you, my dear friend.'

I resolved then and there that I was too young to die and made my way into the woods. The sky and the fields all around me looked beautiful, and that gave me inspiration to live.

'Goodbye, childhood,' I said. And though I was only a short, little girl, I resolved to walk tall, to freedom, to life. 'If I am to survive, I have to start believing that I am very big, and become completely independent, like the animals in the wilds.'

I soon fell asleep and did not feel anything at all for a while. I slept for hours, too tired even to dream. When I woke up from my nap, I felt greatly refreshed and full of new energy.

Autumn was not far away, and I shuddered when I saw the weather changing. I had no coat or umbrella and began to feel a little cold. Within a few days, the rains had begun. It rained a lot, sometimes in sudden down-pours and other times in a fine drizzle. As I was out in the wilds, unsheltered and unprotected, I often felt numb from the cold and damp. I broke off a branch that still had a few leaves on it and was big enough to give me a little shelter. This big branch also camouflaged me so that, from afar, I looked like a small bush among many other bushes. Whenever the leaves of my makeshift shelter withered and turned brown, I would take out my penknife and cut off another branch so that I had a lovely new umbrella at all times. When I had been much younger, I had learned to make many things from branches, not just counting sticks for school. Now, I was glad I had remembered to take my precious penknife.

The air was suffused with the aroma of mushrooms, and the onset of autumn worried me. It was only my determination to outlive my pursuers that reinforced my will to carry on. Although blueberries loaded the bushes and strawberries grew abundantly, I could not satisfy my hunger with them alone, and I knew I would have to take more risks if I were to survive.

The rains had turned the earth to mud, and the forests had changed in appearance. The wind had stripped the trees of their leaves, and they could no longer afford me much protection. But I knew that I had to hide from my would-be executioners who roamed the area like packs of wolves, and I searched for more suitable 'accommodation'. I needed a place where I would at least be sheltered from the winds that were becoming icier by the day.

The terrain was becoming increasingly more difficult to negotiate, and my feet got caught in the mud, which stuck to my shoes. I became concerned about the effect the weather was having on my appearance and how conspicuous I would then be when I entered the villages in search of food. I was happy that I could not see what I looked like, and the animals certainly did not care.

Until then, my shoes had remained serviceable, but they could not last much longer. I knew that it would be impossible to continue walking without them, so I devised a plan to preserve the soles a little longer by tying bits of rags around them. This method slowed down my walking, but I was in no hurry; I had plenty of time. Despite my efforts to protect them, my shoes soon fell apart, and I had to throw them away. I knew that, unlike the animals, I would not last very long in stockinged feet, and I became fearful of stepping on something sharp or even a little snake. But I remained safe, never tripping over logs. I did not even catch a cold. I kept on thanking *Hashem* for that.

I found myself a good place to hide during the day; this was in the middle of a thicket just big enough for me and Malach. I spiked some branches and placed them in front of the 'entrance'. Anyone wishing to enter my hideaway would first trip and hurt himself, and in the ensuing confusion, I would have time to slip away to the other side of the bush. I wondered if my plan was just wishful thinking, but did not *Hashem* say: 'You try, and I will help you'?

I did not have to wonder very long, because a short while later, when I was hiding in that thicket, I saw a dark shadow moving in my direction. I prayed that it was not a partisan or fugitive as I didn't want them to get hurt by my defences. 'Oh, please,' I said to Malach, 'I don't want to hurt innocent people.' I didn't have any binoculars to be able to observe anyone from far away, and I now wished I possessed that precious instrument. I was lucky to be blessed with very good eyesight, but it was quite dark already. The night would not save me, however, for I knew that the Germans possessed quite powerful flashlights. I lay still without making a sound.

I soon heard a man cursing in German as he approached the spot where I crouched. He may have heard the sound of moving branches coming from my direction, because he seemed to sense that there was someone nearby. Perhaps he had unusually sensitive ears and could hear from very far. But even so, he could not have discerned whether the noise came from an animal or from a human being. Of that I was sure, and I tried to relax, having no alternative.

Nearer and nearer he came, and soon he stopped to look in my direction. Surprisingly, I felt no fear, just hate and an urge to hurt him. Though I knew that neither my knife nor any branch would be a match for his gun, I decided to have a go at him with a branch straight in his eyes should he discover me.

It did not take too long, and soon the tall, fat German approached, and I could see that my plan had worked very well for he stumbled and hurt himself on the branches as he fell. It took him a few moments to recover, but he soon straightened himself, and cursing even more vigorously, he headed straight for my hiding place. When he was just a few feet away from me, Malach jumped down from the tree and went straight for him, scratching his face with her claws.

'*Du dumme Katze.* You stupid cat!' he shouted and tried to shoot her.

Malach managed to get away and hide up a tree, as only cats can do. The German looked up at the tree, but he did not take aim. He must have decided to save his bullet for a human being. I smiled to myself and wished he would meet a dangerous animal which would attack him, or better, he would meet one of the partisans who roamed the forest; for they were more dangerous to the Germans than wild animals.

Satisfied that what he had believed to be a human being was only a mischievous cat, he limped away and disappeared into the thick forest. Malach now returned and sat next to me, her bright eyes shining in the darkness. Reassured by her presence, I allowed myself the luxury of dozing off for a few hours again. I would have continued sleeping for a long time had my stomach not reminded me that I needed to eat once more – a sign that I was still healthy and very much alive.

More and more, I became determined to put up a struggle and die a hero's death if need be. I remembered sitting in the back of my grandfather's class and hearing the story of *Chanukah* and the Maccabean revolt and decided that if the Maccabees could fight, then so could I. So what if I was only a young girl with no one to teach me how to do it? 'I am ready to persevere with my struggle,' I said to myself.

I looked at the landscape of undulating fields to which I had become accustomed. 'How lovely is Your universe,' I said as I looked up towards Heaven. 'Thank You, *Hashem*, for allowing me to enjoy the beautiful world You created, and thank You for creating me and allowing me to be so free until now.'

11. Auntie Aniela

I sat down for a little while and pondered what my next actions should be. Instinctively, as if so directed, I decided to walk towards Korchów, the nearest place I knew. I made up my mind not to enter anywhere, even if I was invited in. Instead, I would say I had come to the wrong address.

The first door I knocked at was opened by a very unfriendly woman; I asked her if she was my grand-mother's sister, Reginka Pelowa, knowing full well that she was not.

'You won't find anyone by that name living in our vil-lage,' she said. 'But try next door. Old Mrs Sidorka is ninety years old and knows everyone in the surrounding villages.'

'Does she live on her own?' I asked.

'She lives alone,' the woman answered. 'She'll be only too pleased to have a little chat with you. She might even offer you something to eat as she often does to people who knock on her door.'

I could not believe my ears, as I needed a hot meal right now more than anything else, and I felt that my prayers had been answered once more.

'Thank you very much,' I said to the woman. '*Do widzenia*. Goodbye.' I tried to sound as indifferent as ever, not to arouse her suspicions. I was quite fearful that she might follow me out of curiosity. Though I had straightened my hair with my fingers, I probably looked quite odd without shoes on my feet. But I must have looked convincingly serious to her and very much a Christian girl, which was most important.

Encouraged by the information she gave me, I picked up Malach and went to knock on Mrs Sidorka's door. A very frail old lady opened it. I was glad to see that she looked nearly a hundred years old and almost blind. I embraced her and kissed her on both cheeks, and she returned my kisses.

'Are you Marysia?' she asked. 'Are you my sister's granddaughter? You look so much like my late sister.'

'Yes, I am Marysia,' I replied, 'and I was sent here to visit you and find out if you need any help. I am strong, and I like to look after older people. I love you, Auntie,' I added, feeling quite guilty for lying.

I hoped that I wouldn't be punished for such a grave moral offence, which was quite out of character for me. Mrs Sidorka tried to observe me, but her eyesight was not very good, and I could see that she believed what I told her.

Although this woman standing in front of me had never set eyes on me, she embraced me and kissed me on both cheeks once more, this time without any prompting from me. When she finally let go of me, she said, 'Sit down, my dear, and let me take a good look at you.' She peered at me for a while and suddenly asked, 'Why are you so cold, my dear child?'

'I was foolish,' I told her. 'I did not listen to my mother and went out without a coat or an umbrella. I lost my shoes when I ran away from a wild dog,' I lied.

'My poor child,' she said. 'See if any of my shoes fit you. I have some spare pairs. Are your clothes wet as well? Here, take a dress and a warm jumper of mine. You can borrow my coat for your way home, but you must return it as it's the only one I've got.'

'I won't take your coat, Auntie,' I told her. 'But if you've got a long cardigan, that will do fine. And some underclothes.'

'That's no problem at all. I have plenty of underwear,' she said with a smile. 'I used to make them myself. I live far away from the shops, and it was always quicker for me to make them than to buy them. There are many people going around here selling pieces of material.'

I remembered that my father had been one of the salesmen, but I said nothing. I looked so much like my father, I was glad Mrs Sidorka did not see well.

She was so very small, even smaller than I. That suited me well; except for her shoes, her clothes fitted me, though they were a bit snug. I could see that my prayers were answered once more, and this knowledge gave me inspiration that I had never experienced before in my life.

'Have a piece of bread and a cup of hot milk for now, my dear,' she said, 'and soon I will make us both a nice hot dinner.' Then she added apologetically, 'I'm afraid I have no meat, but I hope you like food cooked with milk.'

'I love it,' I cried joyfully. 'I'll even help you cook it. But first of all, I would like to meet your neighbours, Auntie dear.'

I wanted to make quite sure her neighbours knew who I was before they reported to the authorities that a strange girl had come to stay in their village. I knew that would have quickly got me arrested, and I was not going to make it that easy for the Germans if I could help it.

'Why did the lady next door say that your name was Sidorka?' I wanted to know, for the sign on her doorpost read a different name.

'That is the only name they know me by,' she replied. 'My friends at my previous house used to call me Mrs Sidorka. They knew someone by that name, and it was easier for them to remember. As for the lady next door, it is better that she does not really know much about me or you. She is too inquisitive. I have a few good friends here, but right now, you seem to have been sent to me from Heaven. My good late sister Helena must have intervened on my behalf in the other world. She was always kind, and I loved her. That is why I love you so much, Marysia dear. Now sit down and rest for a while. I fail to understand how a young girl like you could have walked so far.'

I did as she said. After a while, she took my hand. 'Now, my dear,' she said, 'I will take you around to all my neighbours and introduce you to them. There are not so many of them here. This is a small village, and everyone knows each other.'

This information suited me well. The neighbours would soon believe that I was her great niece. Nothing unusual, really. Or would they indeed believe this? And supposing they recognised that I resembled my late father? They would soon report me to the Germans, I feared, but I knew that it would take them some time to ponder over who I really was.

It certainly was a small village, and as I expected, the neighbours made a great fuss over me because they all liked my 'Auntie'.

'How lucky your Auntie Aniela is to have you to look after her,' one of them said.

I was grateful to that neighbour for giving me my benefactor's name.

'You must have been sent from Heaven,' exclaimed another.

'Let me see, you do resemble her a little,' another neighbour remarked. 'You have the same colour eyes, and you are both small.'

'It runs in our family,' I told her. 'We are all short. To tell you the truth, my Auntie Aniela looks so much like my late grandmother, I almost thought it was her, although she died five years ago.' I had learned this piece of information earlier from Auntie Aniela.

'*Krew nie woda*, Marysia,' Mrs Sidorka said. 'Blood is thicker than water.'

'Lovely Auntie Aniela,' I answered, and she embraced me again.

I was relieved when she let go of me, for I was feeling a little smothered. Even so, right then, it was nice to be loved, especially by someone as kind as this old lady. I wished all people were as nice as she was.

After a few days of hot meals and a soft bed, I became afraid that the Germans would not be as easily deceived as the simple village folk. I decided to return to the forests, figuring the Germans would not venture outside in such inclement weather unless someone denounced me. I made sure to take my leave of all the neighbours and told them that I was returning home to my parents, but would be back soon. 'I want to tell them all about Auntie Aniela and how she feels,' I said.

I hated leaving that warm atmosphere, but I knew quite well that it was not safe for me to stay in one place too long.

Before I returned to the forest, I thought I would try my luck at another village and set off along the highway. After I had walked a fair distance, I saw a horse-drawn cart carrying a well-dressed German, complete with white gloves and all. His driver wore a different uniform, which I soon recognised to be Ukrainian. I looked at Malach but she seemed unperturbed, so I continued walking. There were no houses in the distance, and I decided to pick up my cat and, holding her close to my heart for courage, I went straight up to the cart and asked the occupants if they were, by any chance, going to my home village of Majdan, and if so, would they give me and my cat a lift. How I hoped that the Ukrainian wasn't from Majdan, for then he would have known me. But I had no choice and had to take a risk, the biggest risk I had ever taken.

'*Was fragt sie, das dummes Mädchen?*' the German wanted to know. 'What is that silly-looking girl asking you?'

'She wishes to know if I can give her a ride,' replied the Ukrainian. 'Would you mind if she came along with us? We are going in her direction.'

'As long as she doesn't sit next to me with that vicious-looking cat,' said the German.

'Hop on,' said the Ukrainian in broken Polish. 'And mind you, hold the cat tight.'

I promised him faithfully I would and turned to give the officer a big smile, receiving only a frown in return. He seemed quite displeased at my presence but was ashamed to admit it to his driver.

I was very proud of myself that I achieved the impossible. I knew that the worst that could happen was for them to tell me to get off. I quickly thought up a name for myself in case they started asking me questions about who I was. Luckily for me, they did not. The ride passed uneventfully. When I got off, I thanked them politely, holding Malach up to them and waving goodbye with her paw. They seemed pleased to have got rid of me at last – but not as pleased as I was to have got rid of them. I tried to remember how many times I had escaped death, but it was better not to count them. Better to thank *Hashem* for narrow escape and survival once more.

There was no time to rest now, and I had to continue walking. I promised myself a long rest after my ordeal. I was close to the village of Majdan now, and some of the locals saw me alighting from the cart. When I approached them, one of them asked apprehensively, 'How come you got a lift on that cart? Are you a relative of the Ukrainian?'

'Yes, I am,' I lied. 'He is my uncle. Can anyone offer

me a meal and a drink? I still have some way to go until I reach my home.'

I received quite a few offers from the villagers who thought that I was an important person and maybe even a German spy. I took advantage of their reverence and ate as much as I could. I even filled my bag to the top with provisions. I also asked for a bottle of water and received several. The villagers seemed glad to see me go. They also seemed to have been afraid of the German and Ukrainian which surprised me. I had previously had no idea of how the Nazis behaved to the Poles. Now, I understood that many were abused and had to give up whatever the Germans demanded.

The rain had temporarily stopped and, clad in the warm sweater and underclothes that Auntie Aniela had given me, I felt that there was still some enjoyment to be got out of life. I even admired the rustic scenery that I knew so well from my visits to my Uncle Abram and Auntie Goldie's farm. Yes, the world is still beautiful, I thought, and my will to live became even stronger than before.

I was wary of running into the German and the Ukrainian once more. I knew that their job was to ferret out fugitive Jews, and their suspicions would be raised by meeting me on the open road for a second time. I therefore decided to head straight back into the woods as I now had ample provisions for the immediate future.

'Come along,' I said to Malach, but she was already ahead of me, leading the way.

Though my feet hurt, I walked along briskly. I was elated about all the food I had managed to get in Majdan, and I felt great jubilation at having deceived the German and his Ukrainian driver.

Malach and I stayed in the woods for a few days. I was constantly tired but afraid to fall asleep. I was also beginning to feel the cold. Never in my life did I have so much time as I had then. How I hated living in idleness. Eventually, when the food ran out, I went to pay Auntie Aniela a second visit.

She seemed so pleased to see me again that I told her, 'From now on, dear Auntie, I shall visit you often. You are the nicest aunt I've got. Oh, I almost forgot! My parents send you their love, and they want you to visit them soon.'

I knew quite well that Auntie Aniela could no longer manage such visits.

'I am too old to go visiting now,' she said, 'So please continue coming here, Marysia dear. I am going to make you a lovely milky soup with cream cheese once again. How does that sound to you? We shall have a feast together. I don't enjoy eating on my own.'

'I should love to join you, Auntie Aniela,' I said. 'You sit down, and I shall prepare it for us.' She was more than happy to allow me to do it.

'What did I do to deserve you?' she suddenly asked, and we both smiled.

'I have got to go home early tomorrow morning, dear Auntie,' I said. 'But before I leave, I want to tell you something which you must know.'

'What is it, dear child? Tell me why you look so sad. Are you not very happy at home, dear child? Make yourself comfortable and tell Auntie Aniela all about it.'

'My father passed away a few years ago, and my mother remarried,' I lied. 'My stepfather is not very good to me, and I often go hungry. I need help with food as I haven't got any money of my own yet.' I looked at her and asked her beseechingly, 'Please promise me, Auntie dear, that you won't tell anyone about this, especially your neighbours. I'm afraid that my stepfather will find out that I've been talking about him behind his back and kill me. He is good to my mother, but he hates me because I don't want to call him Father.'

I was quite fearful that this good woman would not really be able to keep a secret, and I dreaded what the consequences would then be.

'Did I hear right, my poor child?' she said. 'Come as often as you like, and I will fill your sack with good food. I promise not to tell anyone.'

'In the future, I will have to come here at night, when no one can see me,' I said.

'You are right, my dear,' she replied, and her eyes filled with tears, and soon my eyes began to fill with tears, too.

I began to be fond of Auntie Aniela and felt guilty about deceiving such a gentle lady. I felt bad that I had to ask *Hashem* to help me think of new ways of deceiving such innocent people. I almost began to hate myself for it, but I did it anyway. My feelings for Auntie Aniela were now quite genuine. I embraced her, and she held me for quite a while before letting go of me.

I wondered if she had any other nieces but decided it was best not to ask her; I should have known this myself.

12. The Forest and the Partisans

The next day, I set off once again and walked towards Chmielek. My parents had been innkeepers there for a few years after they married. They left Chmielek after a Jewish man by the name of Balande was murdered there. The culprit was never found. One day, when my mother was alone, a Polish villager came to the inn and started drinking heavily. After he had downed quite a number of drinks, my mother refused to serve him any more. The villager told her that he would do to her what he had done to 'that Jew Balande'. Soon afterwards, my parents moved to Tarnogród.

Now I decided to pay this village a visit, not because I wanted to see it but simply because I needed food. I also wanted to pretend that I was a Christian girl looking for work, for I needed a place for the winter.

Chiemelek was not so near, and I had to sit down and rest several times on the way. While I rested, I ate and drank Auntie Aniela's provisions. Luckily, all the people I met on the road and in the fields believed that I was a feeble-minded Christian girl, which suited me fine. Some farmers even let me help harvest their fields in return for food, usually potatoes which I learned to eat raw after first washing them.

I wandered around Chiemelek and the surrounding

villages for a while. Finding shelter at night was not a problem since there was a haystack in nearly every field. Those haystacks sheltered me from people as well as from the wind. There were small lakes throughout the countryside, so I had plenty of water to drink. I was also happy that I was able to clean my potatoes in the fresh water, and could wash my tattered garments in the lakes, using stones instead of soap to remove the dirt.

After a few days, I became quite fearful about the future that awaited me. I was also tormented by thoughts of my poor family's fate. Hunted like a young animal separated from its flock, I felt desolate and in need of sharing my sufferings with another human being. Desperate, I began to confide in Malach more and more. I hoped that she would continue to be at my side at all times. But I needn't have worried, for she did not look as if she was about to abandon me just yet. Sometimes, I stroked her soft fur and said, 'If only *Hashem* would grant you a proper voice so you could talk to me, how lovely that would be.'

I sat down to think and plan what to do next. I suddenly seemed to be short of ideas.

All of a sudden, I got the urge to return to Tarnogród and see what had befallen my grandfather and the rest of the Jewish people who had remained in the ghetto. I knew quite well that I would be taking a very great risk by going back. A German might see me on the way and shoot me. Or someone in Tarnogród might recognise me and betray me to the Nazis. I was also not certain if the Germans had left any Jewish people alive, but I felt I had to go to Tarnogród once more to convince myself that there was no more future for me among my own people.

I had not quite made up my mind as to how I was going to enter the town or from which direction. I also had to think about where I was going to find food, because I knew that without eating or drinking, I would not last very long. If only I were like my companion, Malach, who never seemed to be thirsty or hungry.

'How do you manage to exist?' I asked my little friend.

But she remained silent.

I took out my small sack which contained a few precious provisions. I still had some pieces of bread and a bottle of milk. An old Polish lady had taken pity on me and given me the food. When she asked why I looked so neglected and unhappy, I told her that I came from a nearby village where I had lived with my cruel stepmother who treated me so badly that I was forced to live out in the fields and beg for my food.

'She treats me like this because I said that my real mother was nicer than she is,' I had told the old lady.

'You poor child,' she said, and a few trickles of tears ran down her cheeks. I was glad to see that there were still people with soft hearts.

'You are a very kind lady,' I told her. Then I lied and said, 'I wish you were my mother.'

I also blessed her for her kindness, something I learned and adopted from the peasants in Łuchów Dolny. Whenever I was given some food, I would always thank my benefactors with, 'May the Lord bless you for your kindness,' and they would reply with 'Amen'. I tried to put on my nicest smile and was always complimented on my good manners. One couple confided in me that their daughter could learn some manners from me, as she never said thank you for anything. One kind lady even suggested that I share her daughter's bed. I needed a good rest and would have been very happy to have accepted, but I knew that it would be too risky. Better to sleep in barns and stables with the animals. I was not afraid of them; I only feared Germans, not animals, who were my good friends. How innocent they all seemed compared to the Germans.

I went back to the forest to allow myself to think about how to enter Tarnogród and stayed for a while. Before long, I became friendly with the deer and squirrels in the forest and loved the peace and tranquillity that existed among the trees. 'Do you want to exchange appearances with me?' I asked a squirrel one day, but it only continued climbing higher and higher, until it disappeared into a hole in the tree trunk.

It was a warm day, and I took advantage of the hours of sunshine to wash my clothes in the lake. I hung them across some branches to dry in the sun and gentle wind.

While they were drying, I hid in the bushes and recited a *Yiddish prayer* my mother had taught me.

I was very tired, and despite my efforts to stay awake, my eyes soon closed. I was awakened by something licking my hand. Startled, I instinctively waved the stick that I had in my hand. After I had fully regained consciousness, I saw a deer running away. I apologised to it for threatening such a peace-loving creature, so different from those German beasts.

How peaceful it was in the forest. Looking at the beautiful surroundings, I suddenly realised that Malach had disappeared. I became concerned and started searching for her. Finally, I saw her, cowering under a tree trunk. 'Why are you hiding under that tree?' I asked, going after her. I grabbed her tail and abruptly froze as I heard the sound of someone coming in my direction. I crouched down as low as I could under the same tree trunk, making sure that my feet were not protruding.

I peeked and saw two mounted SS men riding in my direction. They dismounted from their horses and sat on the ground next to the very tree trunk where I was hiding. Malach did not make a move, and neither did I. They had not seen us, but we were both in danger. I was beginning to get cramp and wondered how long I could hold my position. It would be dangerous for me to make even one move. For the first time, I understood why *Hashem* did not make me grow up very tall, for my feet would then have been sticking out under that tree trunk.

The SS men seemed to enjoy the fragrant forest. They were very pleased with themselves, as though they had accomplished a great feat.

I was quite fearful that I might suddenly feel an urge to cough or sneeze and not be able to hold back, but luckily this did not happen.

They took out some food and bottles of wine and after several swigs began to sing. '*Heute wollen wir alle singen, trinken wollen wir alle Wein.* Today, we all want to sing and we all want to drink wine.'

Swines, I thought. What were they celebrating? How many lives have they taken today?

I felt like taking some branches and hitting them on the backs of their heads. I felt like hitting them many times – one for every person they had killed or tortured. They were by now so drunk, they surely would not have known what had hit them. But, I would leave it to others to punish them all severely for my suffering and my family's suffering. I just hoped that their reckoning would come very soon.

They took some watches and other jewellery out of their pockets and held them up to admire their loot.

'*Ja, die werden wunderbar für unsere Frauen sein,*' they said. 'Yes, they will be lovely presents for our wives.' They must have just removed the jewellery from some Jews they had murdered.

The time must have been later than they thought, because the two beasts abruptly mounted their horses. To my delight, they soon disappeared into the dense forest. I always knew the trees were my friends, but right then, they were especially precious to me. I must have known that they would one day save my life, and I expressed my gratitude to the Almighty for creating them, and getting me used to living near them when I was just a child. I added an extra blessing, 'Thank you also, *Hashem*, for making trees and making them fall down and turn into trunks, for how else could we have hidden under them?'

Making quite sure that no one else was in sight, I crawled out from my uncomfortable position, followed by Malach, who did not have to stretch her tired limbs like I did. 'Thank you for going away and for leaving me alive,' I silently called after the soldiers.

In their haste, the soldiers had left some biscuits behind wrapped up in a bag, and I ate them. 'Thank you also for leaving me such good food,' I called after them again. How I wished that I had a *siddur* or *Tehillim*; then I could say a proper prayer.

While I was munching on the biscuits, I heard something that startled me: it was gunfire. Looking at a clearing in the forest, I saw soldiers shooting at SS men. I was greatly surprised; surely civil war hadn't broken out?

I decided, therefore, that I had to investigate. I made sure to run from tree to tree and constantly hide at the back of one, away from the direction from where the shots came. I climbed a tree to get a better view and looked around. I could see German soldiers lying dead and others disarming them and going through their pockets. I wondered if my eyes were seeing things properly and decided that my vision was fine, as usual.

After the shooting was over and all the SS men had been killed, I approached the spot where other soldiers were resting. I remained hidden, so they could not see me. They all looked like men, but when they started to speak, I realised that some of them were girls. But what language were they using? It didn't sound like German. I strained my ears and heard a mixture of Polish and

Yiddish. Occasionally, they broke into German and sounded like Germans.

I began to put two and two together and soon understood who they really were. They were partisans – Jewish boys and girls dressed in German uniforms, which they had removed from the soldiers they had managed to kill. The original owners of the uniforms must have distinguished themselves in battle as the jackets were emblazoned with decorations. These youngsters were very brave to have tackled such accomplished soldiers. They knew they had very little chance of survival, yet they had made up their minds to kill as many Germans as they possibly could before they themselves died.

Perhaps I, too, could kill a few German soldiers before they killed me. I was overjoyed. I had never expected such a good opportunity and hoped that I would be accepted by the partisans. I decided to try and join them immediately. I plucked up the courage to come out of my hiding place. So as not to frighten them, I quickly started talking to them in Yiddish. They were indeed Jewish, they said, and embraced me, wondering how I could have survived alone for such a long time. I related to them, in short, about my close encounters and good fortune so far.

'If you survive, you will have a very interesting story to tell,' they said, probably not believing for one moment that I had any more chance to survive than they did.

Their leader looked at me kindly and said, 'We have no illusions about our chances of survival. But we are determined to kill as many Germans as we can before we die. You are too young and too small to join us, and your German is not fluent.'

This was the only time that I regretted not being very tall. But I did not care that I spoke German with an accent; I knew quite well what I could have done without uttering one word, for who needs to kill and speak at the same time?

I begged them, told them I was strong and willing to learn, but they assured me that I stood a better chance of survival on my own.

They gave me some hot soup which they somehow had managed to cook. They added some pieces of bread and told me not to share my food with the cat. 'It knows how to fend for itself better than you do,' they said.

'Come to think of it,' I said, 'I've never seen it eat or drink.'

They said it probably went foraging when I slept.

I hugged Malach and said a few words to her. They must have thought I was a strange little girl, but right then I didn't care what anyone thought of me. Feeble or not feeble, I needed someone to talk to, and my cat never interrupted me. It just sat next to me as usual and looked at me with its soft, sad eyes. In Malach I had the most sympathetic listener. We were perfect companions, and no one was going to separate us, not even the kind partisans.

I said goodbye to them and disappeared into the thick forest.

13. The Survivors in Tarnogród

One day, Malach started heading out of the forest. I still wanted to go back to Tarnogród, but I knew that the chances of my slipping back unseen by the Germans were slim. I would just have to take the risk. My brain was momentarily too tired, and I was forced to rely entirely on Malach for guidance. 'Wait for me,' I said. 'I'm coming.'

As we walked side by side along the road, I saw many Polish people that I knew, but none took any notice of me. I tried to recollect what good I had already done in my short life to merit being saved again, but I could not imagine that I had already done enough. Perhaps I would still be able to do a lot of good in the future, if there was to be one.

Fear was now the last thing on my mind. I felt an inner strength run through me and a quiet excitement to walk once more to my dear home town. Had I known what awaited me in Tarnogród that day, I would have hidden in a hole in the depths of the forest, and not gone back to the ghetto.

I decided I would enter Tarnogród after nightfall. I closed my eyes and imagined for a while that I was going home to my dear parents and that my mother would greet me with a hug and make some hot soup for me. I soon realised that I was daydreaming again and decided it would be better to pray. 'Please make all the Germans blind, or make me invisible so that they won't see me entering the ghetto,' I said.

I entered the town, unseen and unheard by anyone. I observed my family's house for a while before approaching it because I did not know who the present occupants were. When I finally walked into the house, I found my old grandfather lying on his bed. He struggled to his feet when he saw me, asking for news of my parents and sisters. Apparently, no one had told him they had been deported. I replied that I had no news either and promised him that one day I would let him know. I was glad that he was still hopeful of the family's return. I kept back the tears and let him keep his hope of seeing them again. It was better that he should finish his days without knowing what happened. How I wished I did not know either, for then I would also still have hope.

People I had never seen before lived in the house now. They were probably refugees from other Jewish ghettos in the area. They all looked forlorn and resigned to their fate. They knew what the Nazis had done to my family and thousands of others like them; they knew that the same fate awaited them in the near future. I had to cheer up those unfortunate people, and I momentarily forgot that I was one of them. I was not in the forest any longer and free like the animals. In a way, though, I was glad for the sense of belonging that engulfed me.

I gave my grandfather a nice piece of buttered bread and a big apple. 'You must be an angel, not a girl,' he said to me as he feasted on the morsels I gave him. I was surprised that he was still well enough to enjoy his food.

'But what is that cat doing in the house?' he asked when he had finished his meal. 'We have no food for it.'

'Don't worry,' I replied. 'It does not ask me for food.'

I played for a short while with the small children in the house, and just for a few minutes, I felt once again like a big sister. Then I stood up and kissed my grandfather, knowing in my heart that he wouldn't live much longer. He was too old and weak to comprehend fully what was happening to all of our people. And I, despite the starkness of my reality, was still too young to take it all in myself, for what normal person could absorb what was happening then?

The Germans had constantly brought other Jews from the surrounding villages to Tarnogród, my Uncle Abram and his family among them. My relatives now lived in the house of Shiya Leib Shister, the shoemaker, who had been taken away with my family. My uncle's brother-in-law, Shimon, and his family also shared the accommodation with them, as well as a woman called Rosie, whose house and shop had been requisitioned and her family taken to Izbice, like mine.

Everyone made a big fuss over me when I walked into the house. 'How could you leave the ghetto?' they asked. 'And where is your Star of David? It's really not safe for you to go without it,' they reminded me.

Soon, their eyes turned to my bundle, and they stopped asking questions. They all knew it contained precious food, but they could not believe their fortune as I pulled out potatoes, carrots, onions, turnips and even a few eggs from my sack. Such luxuries were unheard of in the ghetto now. I could see from their faces that they had stopped thinking about what was going to happen to them later. All they could think of was that they were hungry and that I had brought some good food for them. They forgot their fears and crowded round as if nothing else mattered. Food was the only subject people discussed then; their families were long forgotten.

My Auntie Goldie prepared a hot soup, and I rushed back to my grandfather with some of it. He was delighted to receive such wonderful food and blessed me for it, and then he began praying for my safety. Despite his state of health, he knew that I was courting death by venturing outside after six o'clock. Luckily, I did not meet anyone on the way.

No one questioned me about how I managed to live alone in the forest. I decided that it was best that they should not know everything in case this knowledge would somehow reach the Germans. The Germans might interrogate them and force them to tell the truth.

I learned from my uncle that he and his brother-in-law worked for the Germans, extracting sap from trees. One day, while they were working in the Majdan woods, one of the Ukrainian guards tried to kill a Jew just for fun. The other guards restrained him, and my uncle overheard one of them say, 'Have patience. November 1 will soon be here.'

That meant that the final execution of the Jews of the

area was near. So, with a heavy heart, I took leave of my relatives, fighting back my tears so as not to reveal my thoughts. My uncle thought I was only going out on one of my begging trips and suggested that I leave the cat behind. But Malach just kept on following me wherever I went.

Filled with sadness, I headed for my grandfather's house to take my final leave of him. We embraced, and I kissed him on his cheek for what I knew was the last time. I was thankful that he was too weak and starved to understand that we would never meet again. I looked at him for a very long time so that his image would be engraved in my memory, should I manage to survive.

14. The River and the Raft

I set out in the direction of Korchów, cutting through the forest. By now I had learned which trees offered me and my companion the best shelter. As I roamed through the forest, I saw squirrels, foxes and deer. The deer were loping about from bush to bush, enjoying some wild berries; I wanted to join them in their frolicking, but they took fright and scattered, not knowing who I was. As for me, I believed that I was already one of them and wondered how I could best survive in their midst.

I needed some sleep but noticed that Malach had suddenly disappeared. Looking around, I saw her lying in a nearby ditch. 'You silly fool,' I scolded her. 'You mustn't leave me; I am lost without you.' As usual, my words were met with silence.

I was about to stand up when I saw three German soldiers scouting around in the distance. They must have been short of police dogs or felt sure enough to roam the woods, which they believed belonged to them. I realised Malach was trying to warn me to take cover, so I joined her in the ditch. After satisfying themselves that there was no one in that part of the forest, the Germans continued on their way.

By that time, I could not keep my eyes open any longer and soon experienced that sweet unconscious state of mind of much-needed sleep. When I awoke, I had not forgotten that it was now autumn, and a shiver went through my spine when I reminded myself of the winter that would soon follow. I started contemplating what to do next. I knew that constant planning was now necessary if I were to survive.

I remembered a friendly Pole and his wife who had given me shelter for a while in a small village near Majdan. The Polish couple had no room in their house, so I had slept in the garden, which was surrounded by a high fence. The Pole was a woodcutter, and he needed assistance to fell trees and cut the trunks into firewood or fashion them into coffins. I now decided to try my luck once more and beg them for shelter. Even if he and his wife let me stay only a few days, I would have time to think about what to do next.

I made my way there and offered to help with the tree felling.

'I could have done better with a boy,' he told me on seeing me again. 'But you're a strong girl, and I think you'll be quite able to help me.'

I was happy he accepted me as his helper, and we set out together to the forest. I held one side of a heavy saw in my small hands. The farmer stood at the other end, and we felled trees together. At first, I was quite terrified of that dangerous work, being fearful all the time of being crushed by a falling tree. The slightest mistake would have brought the tree tumbling down on both of us. However, I soon learned to trust the woodcutter's judgement. He had done this work for years and knew at a glance which way even the straightest of trees was leaning.

The neighbours were kept in the dark about my existence. The fence was higher than eye level, and the gate was fitted with a sturdy lock. The neighbours did not catch sight of me during the day, as I always hid in the woodcutter's cart when we made our way to and from the forest. The cart had high sides, and since my arrival the farmer had built them up even higher. On the way to the forest, I lay in the empty cart, snatching a few more winks. On the way back in the evening, I lay down among the logs.

On our return, we had a lovely cooked meal of potatoes, sour cream, soft cheese and plenty of buttered sandwiches. I was quite satisfied to continue like this. However, this good fortune of mine did not last very long.

I was fast asleep in the garden one night. I was well hidden, my straw sack lay against the fence. I woke up suddenly, hearing whispers from the other side of the fence. I overheard a neighbour telling his wife that he was going to climb over to see what the woodcutter was hiding in his house. I became afraid as I knew that he would soon spot me, and that would be the end of me. I knew I had to do something quickly. I could not allow him to climb over the fence first.

Out of nowhere an idea came to my mind. After living in the wilds for so long, I had become adept at imitating dogs. I now put this expertise into practice with resounding success. As the neighbour began to climb his ladder I started, first softly and then more loudly, to bark like a very large dog. The neighbour, on hearing my growls, lost his grip and fell off the ladder. I could hear him and his wife running off.

I could not believe my good fortune and thanked *Hashem* for giving me that idea so quickly. I surprised myself as to how well I had done it.

That commotion woke up the woodcutter and his wife, and I explained to them what had happened. 'What a clever girl you are,' the woodcutter said. Then he went round to the other side of the fence and took the neighbour's ladder into the garden. I wasn't the only clever one.

After that incident, no one came to peek at the woodcutter's house again as the rumour had quickly spread throughout the village that he had a vicious dog. But I soon moved on as I decided it was not safe for me to be there any longer. I could not keep on barking all the time, and I was afraid that the neighbours might try to kill the dog that might attack them one day.

I thanked the woodcutter and his wife for their kindness. They gave me quite a lot of provisions when they realised that my mind was made up, and I bade them farewell.

I did not know where I was going to go next. I only knew that careful planning was necessary since a mistake could cost me my life. I just wandered around, unable to decide what to do. I dozed off near a big tree and slept for a very long time. I awoke refreshed and began to enjoy some of the food given to me by those kind people. It had been raining but now it had stopped, and I did not feel too cold. But I missed that straw sack on which I had slept in the woodcutter's garden. What a luxury that had been!

One day, when I was walking not far from Majdan, I saw something that mesmerised me. There were a great number of tree trunks attached to some crates floating down the nearby river. There was nothing visible to pull them, certainly no motor boat was attached, and I wondered how those trunks were propelled down the river, all in a straight line. Then I noticed that each tree trunk had a rope attached to it joining it to the others. I could not take my eyes off that sight and decided that I had to find out how this was possible. If I could float along the water like the logs, I could give my tired feet a rest. I needed a rest, and here was a great opportunity.

The trunks moved very slowly and gracefully, and I decided to take a chance and have that ride. Bypassers saw me contemplating my jump and warned me that it was dangerous to jump onto a floating log, but I assured them that I was very good at aiming. I stood as close as I could to the water's edge and took a carefully judged leap, landing right in the middle of a trunk.

I then lay down, enjoying the ride and the bright sunshine reflected in the clear water. Soon, I noticed a small bundle lying between two trunks and picked it up. To my surprise, it was a hundred *zlotys* in notes. I felt quite guilty about taking the money and apologised to Malach for doing so. 'I am sure that whoever this money belongs to needs it less badly than I do,' I explained as I hid it safely away in my pocket. I hoped I would still have the opportunity to spend it, but I did not know where that might be. I was not going to any large towns; it would not have been safe for me to do so.

On the way down the river, farmers in horse-drawn carts kept shouting that it was not safe for me to ride on that tree trunk. I shouted right back that I did this quite often and was in no danger at all. The trunks slowed down after a while, and I realised that they were almost at their journey's end. I jumped off onto the grassy river-bank and made my way to the nearby village.

I approached the first house I saw. Taking a five-*zloty* note out of my pocket, I knocked at the door, which was opened by a friendly man. I told him that my uncle had sent me to him to buy food as there was very little to eat in my home town now. He was quite taken by surprise and asked me why my uncle did not come himself.

'He is much too busy,' I told him. 'And I am quite capable.'

'I can see that for myself,' he commented. 'But I still cannot understand why such a young girl as yourself has to carry all those provisions on a long journey.'

I became fearful that he suspected I was not telling the truth.

'What is your uncle's name?' asked the man.

'Janek Wrubel,' I told him. 'He knows you very well, and that is why he sent me to you.'

'I have never heard that name before. Besides, we haven't got much food here either,' he said. Then he saw the note in my hand. 'But give me your five *zlotys* and tell me what you want.'

'I want three bottles of milk, a large loaf of bread,

butter and some fruit,' I told him. 'I see you have a lot of fruit trees here. I wish we had some at home.'

'Where is your home?' he wanted to know.

'I come from Sieniawa. I got a ride here, and I am getting one back. Can you speak Ukrainian?' I asked him sheepishly.

'Not a word,' he replied.

'I can,' I lied. 'I'm Ukrainian.'

This piece of information frightened him. 'Please don't tell anyone that I have so much food here,' he said.

'I won't,' I promised. 'But I may be back for some more one day.'

Before I left the farm, I had the audacity to ask for a hot drink as well. I was sure I would get it because my supposedly Ukrainian origins made me an important person. I saw that he was quite pleased to see me go, and I realised for the first time that Polish people were quite afraid of Ukrainians.

When I had finished off my provisions a few days later, I wanted at first to go back to that farmer to buy more food. But I decided that it was not safe for me to go to the same place twice. If the Germans heard that I had visited, they might set a trap for me.

As the villages did not have signs with their names on them, I did not always know where I was. Since I did not have to go anywhere in particular, it made no difference where I would eventually arrive. But I could not stay anywhere for more than a day or two, and I was constantly at risk when knocking at strangers' doors, for I could be recognised at any time and betrayed. I knew that the most important thing was for me to meet very kind people who either did not care or did not realise who I was. Many times, I sat down to deliberate who I really was to deserve to be hunted like an escaped prisoner. But I always came to the same conclusion. I was innocent, and it was my pursuers who should have been hunted, not I.

I now had ninety-five *zlotys* left in my pocket. I was a rich girl indeed, but I had no home. How I longed to enter one of the houses at night and sit in a well-lit room instead of being all alone in the darkness outside, staring with envy at the lighted windows.

Yet under the great sky, the whole wide world was mine, and I had plenty of time to explore and observe and learn. I became a little scientist and learned to tell the time from the position of the sun. Sometimes, I would assemble a makeshift sundial in a clearing in the woods. I would take a stick and draw a circle in the soil and then place another stick in the middle and estimate the approximate hour from the angle of the stick's shadow. I also learned to observe the direction of the clouds, and if I saw them coming towards me, I knew I had to look for shelter.

I knew that if I were to survive I had to keep myself clean. I borrowed scissors from farmers' wives whenever I did not think they would suspect me and cut my nails. But this was not very often. Sometimes I tried to bite them off, but they were too hard, not having been softened by warm, soapy water. I wondered then if I would ever live to have such luxuries again.

I remembered learning how King David had killed

Goliath, and I wished I had somehow managed to make myself a sling just like he had done. He was a young boy and I was a young girl, so why could I not manage to do the same? I thought about it and realised that I needed elastic, which I did not have. I decided that eventually I too would possess a sling. I would then take cover behind trees or in holes in the ground and kill as many Nazis as I could as they came into range. But I knew that it was only a dream. I dreamed at night, and I dreamed during the day; I had nothing else to do except procure food.

Each time my food ran out, I used the same method as at the first village, buying whatever I could with my *zlotys*. I even bought a pair of shoes from a farmer's wife though they were a couple of sizes too big for me. I told the woman that I was buying them for my stepmother. I still had fifty *zlotys* left, and I continued purchasing provisions from farmers who always believed me when I said I was buying the food for someone else. I had enough money for a pen and paper, but I knew that it would be fatal to be caught with a diary by the Nazis.

I also bought a second-hand watch for twenty *zlotys*. Now I knew the exact time and how many hours of darkness I had to endure at night. I did not wear the watch on my wrist but placed it in the middle of my dwindling bundle of banknotes. I don't need to look at it all the time, I said to myself. It will come in handy at a later date, I'm sure. I believed I would exchange it for some food one day, and I carried on observing the sun, which gave me something to think about.

I returned to the forest and made myself a bed in

some bushes. I don't know how long I slept, but it did not really matter. I felt as refreshed as if I had slept in a real bed. I got up, ate some more of my provisions, picked up my bundle and walked to the clearing. I was pleased to observe that I was still alone.

The days were getting shorter now and the air much cooler. I realised that I wouldn't be able to survive outside in the forest during the winter. I knew I had to come up with another plan, and while thinking, I had something more to eat. Feeling refreshed, I walked on until I entered Chiemelek, the village I knew so well by now. I begged for some food from friendly villagers. I was sure they would not betray me for they had not done so in the past.

I stayed in Chiemelek for a few days, sleeping in a different barn every night, hoping that no one would discover me. Each night before I fell asleep, I listened to the sound of the cold wind blowing through the branches and rustling the leaves. I could not stop thinking about my remaining family. With each passing day, I became more and more lonely until I resolved that, whatever fate was in store for me, I would share it with the remnants of the family.

I decided to return to Tarnogród and began to work out the best approach towards what I still considered my home. I knew that the decision to return was foolish, yet I was so lonely and weary that even a few days with my people and a few nights in a real bed seemed worth the risk. Little did I know what was going to happen in Tarnogród, my beloved town, the very next morning.

15. The Final Round-up

As I approached a small lake, I saw a flock of geese. I cut off a branch from a tree and with it I directed the geese towards an isolated house. On the way there, people looked at me as if I was from another planet, and they began shouting at me to leave those geese alone, feeling sorry for them and not for me. I took no notice of them and kept on dancing around the geese, all the while directing them towards the isolated house. I wanted to investigate who was living there.

The house certainly had been occupied, but whoever lived there had left and the house now seemed deserted. There were indeed a lot of provisions inside as if someone had left in a hurry, or was going to come back shortly. After eating some food on the premises and drinking the milk that I found there, I filled up my sack with food and set off.

I lost my bearings and was unable to find the highway. Soon, I came to a clearing where some Polish lumberjacks stopped their work to ask me how I had got there. I told them that I had left home two days before in search of mushrooms and had lost my way. This prompted them to mention the date: it was October 31. I suddenly remembered Uncle Abram telling me about the Ukrainians in the Majdan woods. 'Have patience,' one of them had said. 'November 1 will soon be here.'

If I was to reach Tarnogród before November 1, I would have to hurry.

As I was walking through Korchów, an old Polish lady gave me some freshly baked biscuits. I did not eat them but stowed them away in my sack along with the food I had found in the abandoned house. I was tempted to give Malach a biscuit but explained to her that my family needed every crumb I could scavenge. Malach seemed not to mind and continued following me, never showing any signs of hunger or thirst.

Though I wanted to reach my home town as quickly as possible, I kept taking different roads to give myself a better chance of escaping detection. I walked fast, sometimes even running a little. It was as if a magnet were pulling me. I changed direction again and was now on the other side of Tarnogród. I had circled the town and found myself on the edge of Łuchów Górny.

Not able to forgo the opportunity to gather more food, I stopped in at some houses and asked the peasants for some. Again, everyone I approached believed I was a Christian girl, but they seemed to think it odd that I had no food. One woman even asked, 'Does your mother not feed you?'

'I live with my stepmother who doesn't like me very much,' I replied.

'Poor girl,' she said. 'Here, have a few eggs. You are welcome to come back here any time you feel hungry.'

I thanked her and promised to be back shortly, but I had a strong sense that my begging days were now coming to an end.

I was now quite well-stocked with provisions, and my sack was heavy. I wanted to sleep for a while near a big tree, but I knew I had to hurry back to Tarnogród to rejoin my relatives. I foolishly believed that somehow my Uncle Abram and Auntie Goldie would be able to protect me, come what may. And I also believed that the Germans could not harm me. They had had plenty of opportunities already and had not yet managed to do so. Perhaps I was still a little naive. I was certainly foolish for going to Tarnogród. I should have stayed away from it that fateful November 1, a day which will be engraved in my memory until I die.

When my beloved Tarnogród came into view, I began racing towards it, as if I had a mission to complete there.

The first thing I did was to go and see my grandfather. He already looked like a skeleton and was desperately hungry, but his happiness upon seeing me was indescribable. I learned then that one can sometimes survive for a while without food, but not without hope. When he saw me, he raised himself with all his strength to greet me. He could not speak above a whisper any more, but he blessed me and wished me a safe journey. I tried to feed him some breadcrumbs dipped in water, but he was already unable to swallow. As I sat near his bed, I saw him fall into a coma. He looked so peaceful, I hoped he would never awaken. He had suffered enough, and there was no chance of him surviving the rigours of the approaching winter. I said a silent, final farewell and went to see my Uncle Abram.

He and his family were also pathetically weak from

hunger. Almost immediately, my aunt made a hot, nourishing meal with the provisions I had brought. After we ate, my uncle told me that those people who had been taken to Izbice at *Erev Rosh Hashanah* had been put into wooden shacks and burned alive. News of the massacre came to light when the *Einsatzgruppen*, Nazi extermination troops, boasted of their 'achievements' in the ghetto.

I stared at him in horror, but he had nothing more to say.

Completely exhausted, I put on a nightgown and cried myself to sleep.

The sound of screaming from within the house and gunfire outside awakened me in the early hours of the morning. I ran to my aunt's sister Gitel, who sobbingly said she envied my parents and sisters because they had all their troubles behind them. The men went into the next room to *daven* and say *Tehillim*. They knew what the shooting outside meant; the final hour had already come. I was quite certain that my time had come at last; that I, too, would die that day.

Suddenly, Auntie Goldie shouted to me to get up quickly and run for my life.

There was no time to dress. I stood trembling in my nightgown while my aunt pressed a basket of bread and some water into my hand. At that moment, a soldier burst in through the door and ordered everyone out of the house. I had no choice but to follow the others, but I had no intention of going to certain death. I decided to escape again.

Signalling Malach, I quickly made my way into the next yard, slipped into a barn and hid under the straw. A minute later, the Christian owner entered with two soldiers. They ordered him to rake the straw, so I immediately came out. Rather than run away, I decided to appear indifferent and pretend to the Germans that I was a member of that Christian family.

With great fear in my heart, I took a chance and threw myself at the Pole, begging him quietly in Polish not to give me away, promising him that I would leave as soon as the soldiers had gone. 'I am so young,' I told him. 'And I want to live. One day, I shall repay you.'

The soldiers did not know any Polish and could not understand what I said. To them, it must have looked like the farmer had hugged me for a second and not the other way around. They must have believed that I was that Pole's daughter and that I had slept in the barn for fun for one of them took the rake out of the farmer's hand and began to prod the straw himself. While he was doing this, I slipped out of the back of the barn with Malach behind me.

After the war, I learned that this barn was later set alight, and all the people who were hiding in it were burned alive.

I walked very slowly, as if I had all the time in the world. Once outside the farm, I strolled nonchalantly across a field, picking up pebbles at random.

'*Gehe nach Hause zu deiner Mutti, du dummes Schwein,*' called a soldier as I passed him. 'Go home to your mother, you silly pig.'

But I pretended not to understand, since Poles did not speak German. As I had come out of a Christian house, the Germans did not know that I was Jewish and even instructed the others to leave me alone, indicating that I appeared to be an imbecile. I was still in my nightgown and my hair was dishevelled, so I could not have looked like anything else. I grinned foolishly and waved to all of them. They waved back, and I continued walking, playing with the pebbles all the way.

I knew the area around Tarnogród like the back of my hand and decided to walk to the brick factory across the field. I paused for a while by the kiln and stared into the furnace, trying to drown out the deafening screams of the people, my relatives included, who were being systematically shot in the town.

Half dazed, I trudged on past a house whose Jewish owners had been taken away at the same time as my parents and sisters. The building looked deserted, and I did not expect to see any signs of life inside. However, as I drew nearer, I heard the sound of a sobbing child. I could not continue without investigating. A child's cry always stirred my feelings. This was a melancholy cry, and I looked inside.

The sight that met my eyes was something that I shall never forget as long as I shall live. In the middle of a bare room sat Auntie Goldie's seven-year-old niece Liebele. Tears were streaming down her pale cheeks, and she looked totally forlorn. She did not move from her position or utter a word when she saw me. She was too frightened.

I went up to her and held her tight. After a while, she stopped crying. I do not think she was in a fit state to recognise me, but I suppose that just the warmth of my embrace comforted her. In a thin, broken voice, she told me that a German soldier had come to her family's house and ordered everyone out of the building. Her mother told her to run away and hide in a Christian house. I wondered if her sisters Etele and Toibelle and their brothers had also tried to escape, but I never met any of them.

Although my heart went out to Liebele, I knew that there was nothing I could do for her other than be discovered with her and die as well.

'I am in a great hurry now,' I lied to that poor child. 'Just sit here, Liebele, darling, your mother will soon come to take you home.'

I kissed the little girl on the head and left the house with a heavy heart. I knew full well that she would not last very long, but there was nothing I could do to help her. There was no one with whom I could leave her, and I was not sure then if I would manage to get away myself. But I was going to try, and I prayed for help. When I left, I could not bear to look back at poor Liebele.

Walking further along through the fields, I came to a bridge. I saw a Jewish boy of about twenty hiding underneath it. In his hands, he held a pad and a pen. He must have been writing for some time, because he had filled many pages. As I came into view, he looked up, startled. He calmed down soon and asked me to hide out with him until we could join up with some partisans. But I knew that two people had less chance of surviving than one lone person, and I declined his offer.

Suddenly, we saw a German soldier, accompanied by a dog, heading towards the bridge.

'Here, at least take my diary with you,' the boy pleaded.

But I was forced to say no to this, too; I knew what would happen to me if I were caught with a record of the Nazi atrocities.

Though I left the bridge in full view of the approaching soldier, he seemed not to notice me. He should have noticed me when I came face to face with him. Maybe he saw me but thought I was a Christian girl, a silly Christian girl with a cat.

As I moved farther away, a single shot rang out. A moment later, I saw the soldier leaving, a cigarette dangling from his lips. For him, killing Jews was just a matter of routine. That poor boy had still had hopes of people reading his record of events. But he had become a number in the catalogue of mounting German crimes against humanity. I wished that the soldier's gun would go off accidentally and kill him as well. That would have been no less than he deserved.

I recalled that my father had once had a very good friend in the area who had given me bread on many occasions, and I headed in the direction of his farmhouse. Though I had been there many times, it now seemed far away. I managed to pick up my feet only with great difficulty.

My eyes were, however, wide awake and took in the whole area. My senses were heightened. The trees were stark and beautiful, and patches of grass that still retained colour seemed more green than ever. I looked at the houses as I never had before, and I became more and more determined not to leave the world yet. I began to run now, not even looking left or right.

Dressed only in a nightgown and looking very much like a feeble-minded Polish girl, I reached my destination. The farmer, a very kind man, gave me a slice of bread and a cup of milk to revive me. He also gave me a white linen sheet in which to wrap myself up, and his wife pushed a scarf into my hands.

'I am going to take a big risk,' the farmer said. 'I want to save your life. Do you think you can take my cows out to graze?'

'Yes, I can,' I told him. 'I'm quite used to cows and not at all afraid of them.'

The farmer and his wife instructed me to make my way to a small woodland on the way to Różaniec and tie the lead to a tree. 'Leave the cows there to graze,' he said, 'and make your way to the other side of the forest. We will somehow manage to get our cows back, if not today, then tomorrow.'

I thanked them for their kindness. 'I shall never forget you,' I told them and hoped they would not suffer because they had helped me.

As I walked the cows to pasture, I tried to appear fearless. I smiled and waved at every soldier I saw, as if to say, 'You don't really want me.'

Had any of them bothered to look my way, they would have seen a strange tableau but nothing of importance to them: a cat making lazy circles around the legs of a queer-looking peasant girl who was holding the chain of the leading cow in one hand and tossing pebbles with the other.

From the top of the hill, I looked down at the village I was running away from, and I could see that the whole town had been encircled by soldiers. There was no escape for the people of Tarnogród, and I doubted very much if I could get away.

I secured the lead as instructed and began to crawl through the dense bushes and undergrowth. When I felt somewhat safe, I looked out of my hiding place and noticed five Jewish men not far from the roadside. I recognised them as friends of my parents whom we children had affectionately addressed as 'Uncles'. They were hiding among the few trees that were growing there in the field.

Feeling very excited, I approached them. They were eager to hear news of Tarnogród. They had left the town the previous day, thinking that the Germans were going to round up Jewish male adults only for execution in the Christian cemetery. Reluctantly, I informed them of what had really happened. They all looked at each other, too stunned to cry, as they realised that their wives and children had all been murdered.

After they recovered from the initial shock, they offered me some food. They told me that they gave money to a Polish woman from Różaniec who brought them food and drink. They invited me to join their little group, but I could not visualise that they really had any chance of surviving. Also, I did not want to be alone with five men. I thanked them for the food and moved on, unsure of my destination.

A short while after I parted company with them, I saw a Polish woman leading a German soldier straight to them. A round of shots was followed by an eerie silence, and I knew that my parents' friends had joined the list of victims of German barbarism.

I turned away from the road leading to Różaniec. The woman who betrayed the five men was from that village, and the thought of going there had become ominous to me. I was now on the road back to Korchów. A ditch ran along one side of the way, and I decided to spend the night in it.

I fell asleep at once, only to be awakened by voices shouting, 'Come here, someone must be hiding here!'

Two German soldiers with powerful flashlights and an Alsatian dog soon came in my direction. Somehow, I was not discovered. The dog, having sniffed all around me, was now standing still, awaiting further instructions. After a lengthy discussion, the soldiers turned away and headed back in the direction of Tarnogród.

16. Respite with the Gromykas

I must have slept for quite a few hours in the ditch, for the sun was rising when I opened my eyes. I had recited my Yiddish prayers before dozing off; I had nothing left but my faith. Not far away stood the houses of Korchów, the village I now knew so well. I was still exhausted from the initial shock of being so close to death, and I dozed off again. When I awoke from the fitful little nap, the weather had turned, and the skies were intermittently lit by flashes of lightning. There was no sense in staying in the ditch much longer, so I set off in the direction of Korchów.

Once again, driven by desperation and thirst, I took a chance and knocked at the door of the first house to which I came. It was opened by a short, kindly old man and his gentle wife. Without hesitation, they asked me to come in. A young woman was sitting stiffly in the living room. She did not seem to feel very much at home, an oddity because she was introduced to me by the old couple as their new daughter-in-law. By looking at her hands, I could tell that she had not yet done any hard work in her life, and she was already about twenty years old. She was very pretty and probably came from a well-to-do home. She certainly could not have survived like I had, I thought.

The couple took me into the kitchen and gave me

food and drink. The old lady told me that their newly-wed son had been sent to Germany for forced labour along with many other young Poles. He had left his wife behind with them, but the young wife was lazy and refused to help run the house. The old lady tried to get her daughter-in-law to be more family-minded, but the young woman merely said she had married their son and not them.

This sad state of affairs suited me fine, for it meant the old couple needed my assistance, and I was only too willing to give it. I certainly was not afraid to work, as long as I had my freedom and food. I quietly thanked my parents for not having spoiled me. My early responsibilities had made me tough.

The old man joined in the conversation, introducing himself as Mr Gromyka. 'I was very friendly with your father,' he said. 'Itzik visited us often. I also came to your house on several occasions. That's how I recognised you as soon as I opened the door. I know that these are troubled times for you and your family, and I want to do whatever I can to help you.'

My parents had had many visitors before the war, but I could not recall Mr Gromyka's face. I realised that he and his wife were still unaware of what had happened in Tarnogród. When they asked me how my family was, I replied that they were fine, feeling guilty for being such a liar. I had to lie, or they would have been too afraid to harbour a Jewish girl. I knew it was not safe for them to keep me, but I hoped they would overlook the danger; I desperately needed to rest for a few days.

Mrs Gromyka suggested that I stay with them since they could do with some help in the house and on the farm. I reminded the couple of the penalty for harbouring a Jewish girl in their house. She replied that they felt sorry for me and were prepared to take the risk. But henceforth, they would call me Marysia, not Mala.

'We are sure that you will like your new name,' Mrs Gromyka said. 'And you have to practise answering to that name only.'

I quite liked my new given name. There had been a Marysia in my class, a sweet Christian girl whom I remembered with fondness. I would not mind using her name. Furthermore, Marysia was the name I had used during my visit to Aunt Aniela, so I was quite used to it.

Mrs Gromyka got busy preparing a meal for the family and asked me to peel some potatoes and carrots for the soup. During the meal, they complimented me on the efficient way I had assisted in preparing the food and at how tasty it had turned out. I started baking some bread when the meal was done. When the loaf was in the oven, Mr Gromyka took me into the cowshed. He was pleasantly surprised to find that I was no novice at handling cows.

Mr Gromyka made me promise that I would not venture anywhere except from the house to the cowshed and back. 'Make absolutely certain that no one sees you at any time,' he sternly cautioned me, 'for your own sake as well as ours.'

I faithfully promised to do so. I was happy to have a roof over my head and a bed in which to sleep, even if the bed was only a bench with a straw mattress and my cover a big shawl. The Gromykas were benevolent people; I considered myself lucky for the time being, and I recited my prayers.

After milking the cows, I washed the dishes and cleared them away. I felt quite exhausted, and my eyelids began to droop. I tried to stay awake and think up some more plans, but my eyes closed of their own accord.

I woke up a few hours later, feeling refreshed and surprisingly strong but also guilty for being alive when my entire family and everyone else I had known were now dead. I had to touch myself to be sure that my body was still warm, and I pinched my arm to feel some pain. I also missed Malach, whom the Gromykas would not allow into the house. They said she did not belong to me and that I had plenty of other things to worry about. The cat was probably outside the cowshed feeling miserable in the heavy rain. I honestly felt for her as if she were a member of my family; she was the only family I had left now.

I could not fall asleep again for fear of suddenly hearing a loud knock at the door and the familiar shout of '*Aufmachen! Wo is das jiddiches Mädchen!* Open! Where is that Jewish girl!' But no one called, and I was almost asleep when I felt someone stroking me. There seemed to be fire in the eyes that were staring at me. It was my dear cat, and I could see sadness in her eyes. Crying softly, I finally fell asleep.

I woke up quite early the next morning and soon heard Mrs Gromyka call out, 'Marysia.' I answered without even having to think about it. I was astonished to find how quickly I became accustomed to my new name and new surroundings. Why, I felt quite at home already and even allowed myself to recite a *berachah* over the food that had been set out for me. This I did out loud, for everyone to hear.

'You keep on praying, my child,' Mrs Gromyka said, 'and things will work out for you. But you have to milk the cows before you eat breakfast.'

I quickly picked up the milk buckets from the yard and started walking towards the cowshed, not daring to look right or left. I honestly believed that if I saw no one, no one could see me, especially if I hid my face under my big scarf. Much later, I realised how naive and childish I had been to think so.

I managed to milk both cows without spilling a drop of milk or getting kicked. Proud of my achievement, I returned to the house. I was at last given my breakfast of black bread, cream and cottage cheese. I diced a spring onion and added it to the cheese. As I ate, I felt the strength returning to my tired body, and I thanked *Hashem* for the lovely food. I wondered what I had done to deserve such treats. I resolved to enjoy life while it lasted. It was very precious to me. 'I am only at the beginning of it,' I said to myself.

Despite my newly acquired life of luxury, I knew I had to plan ahead and think of other hiding places. The Gromykas' house could only afford me temporary respite from my wanderings. I kept those thoughts to myself. I decided to wait a few days until I'd had several nights' good sleep and felt a little stronger. I also had resolved to eat as much as I could and thus store the energy inside me, like camels store water in their humps before going into the desert. Before leaving, I would ask the Gromykas for some provisions for a few days, and I was certain they would grant me my wish.

The next day started in the same way as the first, with my milking expertise improving by the minute. The Gromykas seemed to like me, and I saw that they felt very sorry for me. I felt sorry for them too, as I knew what would happen to them if I were discovered on their farm.

Only a few days later, I was walking towards the cow-shed with my face behind the big scarf, daydreaming about meeting other young girls with whom I could converse. Suddenly, I heard footsteps coming in the direction of the cowshed. Looking up, I saw a farmer who lived nearby. His face was as white as a sheet, and he was very agitated; he looked like he had seen a ghost.

'Please believe me,' he said. 'I didn't betray you. I saw you on the very first day you arrived here, but I didn't tell a soul, not even my wife and children. I like the Gromykas and didn't want them to get into any trouble. I don't want to see anything happen to you either, you poor child. But someone else must have seen you and given you away.'

He pressed some food into my hands and told me to run for my life as fast as I could as he had heard rumours that Germans were coming to arrest me. I became dumbfounded and could not even manage a 'thank you', which he so truthfully deserved.

There was no time, however, to think or to lose my head. I began to pray that *Hashem* would help me once again and hurried out through the back yard without going back to the house for my few belongings. As I cleared the cowshed, I saw a woman leading a German soldier into the very yard which I had left only seconds earlier. How they missed seeing me in broad daylight I shall never know.

Noticing a little shed outside the farm, I took shelter there, expecting to be discovered at any moment. It did not take long before I heard shots coming from the direction of the Gromykas' house. I resisted the urge to run back to help them. There was no point; I knew that those kind people were probably dead already.

It is unlikely that there is any other written account of the tragic events of that day; so I venture to record my testimony and pay homage to the heroism of Mr and Mrs Gromyka and to express contempt for the traitors who betrayed me in exchange for a kilogram of sugar – the price paid by the Germans to informers. It is possible the Germans also shot the informer when they could not find me, the truth of which I shall never know. But I still remember Mr and Mrs Gromyka and shall cherish their memories forever.

It was dark in the shed, but after my eyes got accustomed to the dim lighting, I spotted something hanging on a hook. It was a fur-lined man's coat. In one of the pockets was a bottle of water, and in the other, some dried bread. I guessed from its small size that it had belonged to Mr Gromyka. There was also a green kerchief with flowers, and a shawl with fringes, similar to the one I had used as a blanket. On my feet were Mr Gromyka's thick knitted socks which Mrs Gromyka had given me as I had no more shoes to wear and she had none to spare. The shoes I bought in Majdan had long become too tattered from my long walks. They were much too large, which made it difficult for me to run. Right then, running would not have helped me. As a matter of fact, when the time was right, I would have to walk slowly and pretend that I was a free person, not a fugitive.

In the meantime, I tried to make myself invisible in the shed and covered myself with hay, hoping I would not be discovered if the Germans decided to enter my hiding place. I did not dare to pick myself up, not even when I remembered that Malach was outside. Right then, I only managed to worry about myself. After a few minutes of waiting, no one came to investigate the shed. Slowly, I picked up my head and saw my cat sitting at the entrance to the shed, as if to say, 'This is my master's house; no one is allowed to enter here.'

I looked at my watch and saw that it was long past my breakfast time. I took a bite of the dry bread, thinking of the poor Gromykas who would not need it any more. Then I fell asleep.

Malach was meowing outside the shed when I awoke. I wondered about my next step and how long my luck would last. I did not know and did not wish to know either. I was alive, and every moment was precious. I resolved to count my life in days, not years from then on, hoping to count many thousands. And if I managed to live, I would tell the whole world what had happened. I would make sure never to forget the events that had overtaken me, my family and my people. I would make sure the whole world remembered what the Germans had done. I desperately wanted to survive even if it was only for that purpose.

17. A Last Look at Tarnogród

After some time, I left the shed and walked towards the open road. I found myself making my way back to my home town. It should have been the last place in the world for me to visit, but something drew me to it like a magnet. I kept on walking towards my beloved birthplace.

I stopped at the outskirts of Tarnogród and went to the house of Mr Noryca, the man from whom my father had leased his orchards. Mr Noryca was also our postman, and he had seemed just as happy as my grandfather when delivering post from Palestine from Uncle Shmuel. He was always nice to everyone. He was another righteous man who should never be forgotten.

Mrs Noryca opened the door. Her daughter Nadia sat in plain view. Nadia had been a friend of mine, but now she did not even come to the door. She only sneaked a quick look from a distance. Her brother, however, quickly came over to where his mother and I stood, brusquely reminding her that it was dangerous even to speak to me.

Mrs Noryca brought out some food for me and, in a kind manner, asked me to leave. After a moment, she called me back and pointed me in the direction of a nearby house.

'Over there lives a family whose daughter has been called up to work in Germany,' she said. 'They are desperately unhappy about it. You don't look Jewish, Mala, and your Polish is excellent. Perhaps they will send you to Germany instead of their daughter. Please, my dear, don't tell them that I sent you. Just say you heard about it from someone else. May the Lord be with you, poor child.'

I thanked Mrs Noryca though I did not have much hope of a successful outcome to her plan. I took her advice anyway and knocked on the door indicated.

A frail-looking girl answered my knock.

'Can I speak to your mother or father?' I asked her.

Her mother recognised me immediately and did not invite me in. I told her I had heard about their predicament and thought it would be a good idea if I reported to the German Labour Exchange in place of her daughter.

The girl's face immediately lit up. 'Yes!' she exclaimed. 'Who knows how they are going to treat me there?'

With her mother's permission, she went to bring her call-up papers, a letter from the local priest and her birth certificate which all the conscripts had to produce at the Labour Exchange. I read the priest's letter in which he assured the Germans that the bearer of that document was a Christian girl that he himself knew.

They gave me some soup which tasted much better than anything I'd ever eaten before. But while I was happily drinking the hot nectar, the girl's father came home and began shouting.

'What is she doing in this house? Get out!'

As he threw me out into the street, he said, 'You're very lucky that I'm not reporting you to the German authorities.'

As I turned away, I could hear him explaining to his wife that they would have been in serious trouble had the Germans discovered the deception. But the information that I received in that house was very useful to me. I had learned that their daughter was to report to the Labour Exchange in Biłgoraj, the large town nearest to Tarnogród. I planned to make my way there even though I did not have any of those vital documents, nor a way of obtaining them. But I had nothing left to lose.

I continued on toward the heart of Tarnogród. I was sure people were bound to stop and stare at me, a peculiar girl in a man's coat that was about three sizes too big, a heavy shawl over it, an outsized scarf and a pair of thick socks on my feet. I prayed that *Hashem* would make me invisible.

Then, with Malach trotting along beside me, I entered my beloved Tarnogród for the very last time. Automatically, I walked in the direction of my family's house, as if in a daydream. I almost called out: 'Mother dear, please come and help me. Balla dearest, please advise me what to do next. You are much older than me and much wiser.' I said these words quietly as if in a deep dream, from which I suddenly awoke. A shiver ran down my spine when I realised where I was heading, and I instantly changed direction for the town centre.

The familiar streets were quiet and deserted. Tarnogród was peaceful and desolate – almost like a cemetery.

All the people I knew and loved were gone. Only I remained. Momentarily, I began to regret having returned to Tarnogród and thought how foolish I had been to go there. Oh, why did I have to come here once more? Did I not witness the destruction of my loved ones?

'Why didn't you direct me to turn back sooner?' I said angrily to Malach and soon felt guilty for blaming her. I should have known better; after all, she was only a cat.

'Please stay with me,' I said to her. 'You're all I've got now.' I saw that she made no move to leave me, and I felt reassured. To make doubly sure that she was near me when I needed her most, I picked her up and carried her along, holding her tight.

From a distance, I saw a familiar figure. I shivered when I recognised my classmate, Irena. I could see that she recognised me too, for she kept coming towards me.

'Mala, my dear!' she exclaimed. 'What are you doing here? All the Jews have been executed here in the square, and others lie buried in two mass graves.'

All around me were clothing and religious articles, lying on the ground. No one had picked them up, probably because most of them were in tatters. Or perhaps people had been afraid that their previous owners would come to haunt them at night and ask them why they were wearing their clothes. Whatever the reason, no one had cleaned up since the massacre, and it was eight days later!

Irena started crying suddenly. Her tears surprised me, because I did not think she cared too much about what had happened to the Jewish population. Soon, I learned the real reason for her tears; her mother had died only the day before. I embraced her, and she calmed down after a while. Can anyone better understand what it is like to lose a mother? I thought to myself. Yes, I felt sorry for Irena, but I wondered if she felt as sorry for me. With a father like hers it was a little too much to expect, for he was a brute and an informer.

'My father has now taken over the soft drinks shop that used to belong to the Jewish people,' said Irena. 'Come with me, Mala dear. You probably need a drink.'

'I would love one,' I told her and followed her to the shop.

As soon as her father saw me, he grabbed my hand, intending to drag me off to the Germans and collect a reward for denouncing me.

It was only when Irena pleaded with him and began crying uncontrollably that he let me go. He did not pity me; he felt sorry for his daughter who had just lost her mother. Instead of betraying me to the Germans, he gave me some ice cream.

I left the shop and walked further into the market-place. There, too, were heaps of belongings of the Jewish people who had been taken away and executed. There were articles of clothing, prayer shawls and *tefillin*, some of which were bloodstained.

I saw a queue outside a milk shop and joined it though I did not have any more money. When my turn came to be served, the shopkeeper chased me away, telling me to get some money from home first. However, a man standing behind me chastised her heartlessness. 'Have you no shame?' he asked. 'Have you no pity for a young girl who hasn't even got shoes on her feet?'

Embarrassed, the shopkeeper gave me a large ration.

I smiled to myself; I knew the man so well, and he did not recognise me. I wondered what I looked like now. Although I had no mirror, I was sure of one thing – that I looked very odd.

Walking on to the end of the town, I saw a signpost which read 'Biłgoraj 21 kms'. It was raining heavily now, and my feet were numb with cold. But cold or not, document or no document, I knew I had to proceed to Biłgoraj. I simply did not have anywhere else to go.

A short way down the road, I passed the cemetery where a couple of German soldiers were taking a Jewish couple into the graveyard. It was our local grocers, Kalman and Peshi. I recognised them immediately, for I had visited their shop many times when I ran errands for my parents. They also recognised me at once, for they kept on looking back in my direction. I wondered what had happened to their children. I understood that Kalman and Peshi must have been found hiding, perhaps under floorboards or in a tunnel somewhere. But it appeared that they would not be alive much longer. I almost called out to the Germans to take me along with them, but something kept me back. My time had not yet come.

I felt tired and sat down to rest for a while, taking in the familiar surroundings of my almost-forgotten childhood days. I feel ashamed to say that I still enjoyed the beautiful scenery around me. Even in the dim light, with rain pelting down on me, the world seemed beautiful. It was as aesthetically appealing as it has always been, only the people around me were different now.

I was awakened from my daydreaming by the sound of shots coming from the direction of the cemetery. Those swine had executed our grocers. Would they now see me on their return and wonder what a young girl was doing out on her own on such a rainy day? But though they looked in my direction, they ignored me.

Had I become invisible? I knew that the world still had some good people and hoped that they were not invisible. 'Please reveal yourselves to me!' I implored.

It was so strange to be alone, a young girl and a cat.

'This is no time for dreaming,' an inner voice told me.

I soon awoke from my reverie and reminded myself that I still had to go to Biłgoraj to try to mingle with the Christian girls.

18. The Labour Exchange

I stood at a junction and wondered if I should take the high road to Biłgoraj or follow a more roundabout route through the fields.

'Tell me which way I should go,' I asked Malach.

To my horror, she was nowhere to be seen. She had left my side for the very first time. But why? I asked myself. I could not think of an answer. Now, I really felt forlorn and more lonely than ever before. I suddenly lost my confidence.

I had never been to Biłgoraj, so how would I find my way? How would I locate the Labour Exchange? I would have to ask for directions from many people, and they would probably begin to wonder why such a young girl wanted to go to Germany in the first place and why there was no parent accompanying her. I would have to think of an excuse, and I began to prepare what I would say.

I was now devastated by my companion's sudden disappearance and, in desperation, turned back to look for her. Suddenly, as if out of nowhere, a horse-drawn cart pulled up right next to me. The peasant driver asked me where I was going, and I quickly informed him that I had to report to the Labour Exchange at Biłgoraj as I had been conscripted for forced labour in Germany.

'Hop on my wagon,' the peasant said. 'It is market day

there today, and I've got some business to attend to in town. Biłgoraj is twenty-one kilometres away, and you'll never make it by foot, especially without shoes.'

As we rode along, he gave me an apple and some bread; soon he started singing as if to cheer me up. We passed another cemetery, and he pointed out some people who were still burying Jews who had just been executed. He started questioning me about my parents, and I told him that I only had a father and a stepmother. I went into a long tirade, cataloguing her meanness: she treated me very badly; she would not even give me any belongings. Although I was going to Germany for a very long time, she said the Germans would have to buy me some clothes.

'Well as long as you are not Jewish, my dear, everything will be fine,' he said.

He then asked for my home address. He would pass through my home town on his return journey, and he would tell my father that he had seen me and that I was well. He added that he would give my stepmother a dressing down that she would remember for the rest of her life. 'Fancy sending a child to Germany without any luggage or shoes.'

The peasant felt sorry for me and offered to take me all the way to the Labour Exchange as he was sure I would never find it myself. He never once asked me or anyone else where the place was. He seemed to know it quite well, which surprised me. I had no address and would certainly not have arrived there without his help. I was, therefore, most grateful for his kind offer.

'You must be sent from Heaven,' I told him, and I really believed it, for I had not seen him coming from the distance until he was right in front of me. He gave me a friendly smile as if he had known me for a long time and said nothing.

It happened to be the day when the Germans massacred the Jewish population in Biłgoraj. As we reached the town, we saw many people running and being shot down as they tried to flee. The peasant told me that it was a good thing he would be dropping me off right by the Labour Exchange, or I might have been shot by accident.

When we arrived, he gave me some bread and cottage cheese and wished me good luck, repeating his promise to give my stepmother an 'earful'. I knew quite well this would be impossible since I had given him a fictitious address. I also wondered why he had not questioned me, because he had indicated that he knew Tarnogród well.

I bade farewell to the kind farmer and climbed down from his wagon. As he drove off, I looked longingly after him. It had been a relief to feel safety instead of fear for a while. And it had been good to talk to someone who could reply. I had badly needed someone to talk to after listening to Malach's silence for days. But now even Malach was gone.

I began questioning the wisdom of having come to Biłgoraj. Maybe I should have stayed in the woods near Aunt Aniela. It was too late for regrets, too late to turn back. I would never have made it through the massacre in the streets. Even if I had, I would not have managed to survive the winter in the forest – of that I was sure. However, right then my situation seemed hopeless, and it was hard to visualise my freedom.

The drab waiting room at the Labour Exchange was filled with boys and girls. I sat down next to a girl who immediately moved away. Someone else took her place, but after a minute she, too, moved away. It was not difficult to understand the reason. It had been over a week since I had last washed. My fingernails were long and dirty, and travelling on the peasant's cart had not improved my 'aroma' much. Odd as I looked, I began to feel fearful that the Germans would not accept me for work.

I entered one of the toilets, where I drank some water from the tap and washed my hands and feet. I also made a fair attempt to straighten my hair, which had grown very long by then. Using my fingers as a comb, I managed to fashion my hair into a bun. I believed I now looked tidy, even if quite strange. I was still wearing a man's coat, which was much too long for me; under it, I wore only my nightgown and a pair of men's socks without shoes. I knew I looked very conspicuous. At the same time, I had to try and help myself. Now was not the time to give up; I knew quite well this would be my last opportunity to survive.

When I returned to the waiting room, one of the girls complimented me on my good diction and offered me a chair next to her. She asked about my strange attire, and she seemed sincerely distressed to hear that I had such a cruel stepmother. She added that it might be better for me now that I had been called up. Soon, she was summoned into the office. She took her papers from her handbag and said she was happy that we would be together.

'Have your papers ready,' she said. 'They'll call you soon. You're next in line.'

They did not call me, and my mind began to race. To get to Germany, I would have to outwit them, and to outwit them, I would have to be called in and interviewed.

I said my prayer quietly, got up and began staring at the others as if they, not I, looked queer. Many began to look away from me. I was not even worth bothering with, they might have decided. But I knew that I had to bother them – or at least one of them – in order to get some necessary help right then.

Once again, I felt so foolish for going to the Labour Exchange without identity papers to present to the policemen in charge of conscription. Thoughts of Malach came to my mind. Perhaps I had been wrong to accept the offer of a lift into town. Instead, I should have continued searching for my cat. Now I was going to be punished for abandoning that extraordinary cat in the rain.

I stopped thinking like that when I realised I was giving up hope. I must still trust in *Hashem* as I had done until then. My fate was in His hands and no one else's.

Looking around the waiting room, I noticed one girl who looked older than the others. I also thought she looked a little Jewish, and as soon as her neighbour got up, I moved to sit next to her. I could see that she had a frightened look in her eyes, and she became agitated when I tried to talk to her. She began writing something and told me to find someone else to talk to, someone my own age. Despite her unfriendliness, I decided not to leave my chair. My character was such that when I started something, I did not give up so easily; this, after all, seemed my only opportunity. It was a matter of life and death for me. I had to find a way to talk to her alone.

After a while, she got up to join the queue which had formed outside the toilet. I managed to get in right behind her. When her turn came to go in, I pushed myself inside the cubicle with her. She tried to stop me, but I was a very strong girl with an even stronger will. I had not survived all this time only to give up now.

Soon the girl started yelling and shouting at me to get out. Without wasting a second, I named all the objects in the toilet in Yiddish. I knew that if she was not Jewish herself, she would not have understood one word of what I was saying.

Meanwhile, someone outside had heard the commotion and went to get help from a police officer. He knocked at our door and demanded to know what was happening. By then, the girl realised that I was Jewish and assured him that all was well.

Then she looked at me in disbelief. 'You look just like a Christian girl,' she whispered. 'I wish I were that lucky. The fact that you recognised me as being Jewish is a bad sign. I hope no one else will do the same.'

We embraced as if we were sisters or old friends and

allowed ourselves to cry a little. I felt momentarily as if I had got rid of a big load from my chest but knew that I needed a miracle. Soon I would be left on my own. Without documents, I would be arrested and that would be the end of the brave girl. No one would ever know that I had even existed. I had to try harder and without wasting one more moment, or else the girls outside would become suspicious.

I quickly explained my predicament to her and told her that I knew that my fate would soon be sealed. I fully understood, I told her, that she could not share her papers with me as it was not possible to cut them in half, but I hoped that, being older and therefore much wiser than I, she could perhaps offer me some good advice.

She confided that she came from a town called Janów. She had managed to escape from the ghetto when the Nazis destroyed it, killing all the occupants – men, women and children. She had also lived alone in the forest for a little while before deciding to take this one last chance. We realised that we had both survived so far only by taking chances, but this was the biggest risk we had ever taken. There was to be no other chance for us. Either we would succeed, or we would both die very soon. Perhaps they would shoot us.

But what she told me next brought back some hope.

'I haven't got any papers either,' she said. 'I am going to tell them that I come from Pikule, a little village near Janów, where Polish soldiers still held out in the nearby woods after the occupation. The Germans punished the whole village for not betraying those partisans by dousing

Pikule in paraffin and setting it on fire. I am going to tell the police that I was in Janów at the time and that the entire population perished in the flames, except for me. You can tell them the same.'

I sincerely hoped the police officers would believe our incredible story. I must admit that I doubted it very much as I imagined that the police appointed to such a high position were no fools. But there was no alternative, and I hoped for a miracle once more.

Since we were now supposed to have known each other from Pikule and she was supposed to have been my friend, it was natural for us to enter the interrogation room together. She knew all the facts, so I would not have to be questioned separately.

Much to our surprise and relief, the police officers took pity on us and told us they would see what they could do for us.

Suddenly, Malach appeared out of nowhere, as mysteriously as she had disappeared. How delighted I was when I saw my dear cat again. I stroked her fur and did not mind very much when everyone believed I was not quite normal in travelling to Germany with a cat.

Back in the waiting room, a policeman addressed the other conscripts, telling them of our unfortunate plight and about what had happened in Pikule. I was greatly surprised, for I had not previously seen a German feeling sorry for a non-German. The policeman then told them that we had no luggage because we had lost everything in the fire. He was sure, he said, that the other boys and girls could spare a few articles of clothing and that it would be a splendid gesture of solidarity which would stand them in good stead when they got to Germany.

'You can give them food and clothing, but you cannot give them back their families,' he told them, upon which we both began to cry uncontrollably, for unfortunately this was fact, even if it had not taken place in Pikule but in another hell.

To our great relief and delight, they all responded with eager willingness. The boys gave us some fruit, and the girls showered us with clothes. One girl presented me with a small suitcase containing a few items of underwear. Unfortunately, no one could spare a pair of shoes or even a dress. We were overwhelmed by their generosity and grateful for our good fortune.

Now I had someone with whom to share my sorrows and a shoulder on which to cry. Since we were supposed to be the only survivors of our families, my tears did not raise any suspicions. I did not seem so odd any longer, now that everyone understood why I had no shoes or clothes. My friend and I mixed freely with the others; we even became the centre of attention. They all stared at us but this time with caring smiles. My future looked momentarily more secure.

The other Jewish girl, whose real name I never managed to find out, explained to me that we had to be very friendly to all our benefactors. We had to pretend to be very happy and promise them to reciprocate after the war. We even asked them all for their addresses. Since we were not supposed to have any more family, we did not have to give them ours.

'Let's pretend to be confident,' I said. 'We must not appear sad any more. We are young, and young people are supposed to get over tragedies quickly.'

How I wished this were true. We were still very fearful, but for the time being, we had to act. The only time we showed any sadness was when the others began singing '*Mamo, od ciebie dziś z dala*. Mother, I am moving away from you today.'

The following day, we were taken to Zamość, a larger town than Biłgoraj, where the Germans had their headquarters. We were permitted a few hours of leisure and used them to go sight-seeing. I had heard about Zamość before the war, but I hadn't expected to visit it under such circumstances. The sun shone brightly, and I revelled in my temporary freedom. It was nice to be part of a group again, even though the other members were strangers to me.

We passed through deserted streets with only a handful of frightened-looking civilians. Small groups of soldiers patrolled the desolate town. The pogroms must have taken place there only a day or two earlier, for while all the Jewish houses were closed, they did not appear to have been ransacked yet. Obviously, the Germans hadn't had time to do any looting, and Poles could only take 'leftovers'.

I overheard a couple of soldiers discussing the world situation and how everything was going well for them, '*Gott sei dank*. Thank goodness.' The words were a sacrilege coming from them.

I held my newly acquired friend's hand very tightly, and we told each other what we had endured in the last few years. She told me that, at the end, some of the people in her town had been too weak to think clearly. Those people had also believed they were needed for important work in a new place, where they would receive double rations. The majority of the intelligent people, however, had not really believed that the Germans were telling them the truth. They had been suspicious but had no alternative but to go along with them.

Resistance had not been possible, since the young and strong had long been killed. They had allowed themselves to be taken to the cemetery where they were shot, hoping that by sacrificing themselves, their families would be saved. My new friend had not trusted the Germans at all, and she alone somehow managed to leave before they took away the remaining population of Janów. She had escaped death a few times since then.

We soon had to stop talking about the past and think about the future. Fearful that we might meet up with someone who knew us, we thought it wiser to part company. If we stayed together, we might be lulled into complacency. We had to remain alert. The slightest mistake could have been the end for us. It would be safer for us to mix with the other girls from then on.

When we re-entered the waiting room of the building, we were handed a lunch of some tasteless soup and a slice of bread which we enjoyed for we were starving. Then, after each girl was fingerprinted, she turned in the documents she had earlier produced. In return, she received her new identity cards and was ready to travel to Germany.

We were the last to be called in. By that time, we had become very concerned and feared the worst.

Luckily, my friend was called first. They did not ask for her papers, only her name and address. She gave them a Polish name, and I quickly racked my brain for a good pseudonym for myself. I had known someone called Stefania Iwkiewicz at my school, so I adopted her name. To our great joy and relief, we were both given the same kind of identity card as the others had received against their three valid documents. The identity papers were valuable to all the others, but priceless to us. We heartily believed that nothing could go wrong now, and I kept on looking at my identity card again and again with disbelief. I knew that other Jewish girls in Tarnogród had paid so much money for such documents, and they could not use them in the end, and we had paid nothing for ours. I felt my cheeks glowing with happiness, but I still felt guilty that I alone had been given a chance to survive.

After a short stay in Zamość, we were taken to Lublin, where we joined many other youngsters who were waiting for trains to take them to Germany. I looked around for my Jewish friend, and with sudden dismay, I saw her being led away by a policeman. Trembling, I realised that someone had recognised her in such a large town and was suddenly fearful that someone would soon recognise me, too.

In a room at the station sat a girl alone, so I asked if I could join her, as I believed I would be safer away from the crowd. She shrugged her shoulders impassively, so I sat down opposite her. Considering the way I looked, I was not in the least surprised that she did not want to sit near me. Who ever heard of a girl being dressed in a man's coat and having no shoes on her feet? She would have something to tell her friends one day, of that I was certain. I quite understood her behaviour as I would not have acted differently had the situation been reversed. However, my only worry was lest someone from my town suddenly appear. My identity card would then be useless.

I decided to lie down and have a little nap in order to refresh my brain so as to be able to think more clearly. It was, however, too noisy as many youngsters decided to sing to cheer themselves up. They were all sad to leave their loved ones behind and travel to the unknown. As for me, though I was far from happy, I had not felt so safe in a long time.

After a while, we were told to enter some small rooms. I joined another girl, and we started a friendly conversation, but she soon left the room. I had previously noticed a large mirror on the wall, and I stood up to tidy my hair, arranging it with plaits the way I had worn it in Tarnogród. The girl returned to the room and started to give me nasty looks, which made me feel very uneasy. I could see that she was not satisfied with the way I now appeared, unlike previously, when I looked like a poor, neglected village girl. She kept on staring at me with hostile eyes, and an enormous fear began to engulf me. The feeling of safety had suddenly left me.

'Where do you come from?' she soon asked.

I did not think that it was yet safe to volunteer my newly assumed home address, and I asked her in a very friendly manner why she wanted to know. Did she by any chance think that I was one of her relations?

'Most certainly not,' she retorted vigorously.

I could see I was in big trouble now. My cat suddenly appeared, wanting to play and pretending to scratch me; then she went over to the girl and sat staring at her.

'What are you doing here?' the girl shouted. She waved her hands wildly, but the cat did not move.

I deliberately did not glance at Malach and tried to appear indifferent. The girl continued staring at me, and I began to think that she was also from Tarnogród and knew who I really was. However, I soon found out that this was not the case, but what she said next made me shiver.

'Now that you have rearranged your hairstyle,' she said, 'you look like a *Żydówka*, a Jewish girl.'

Saying so, she quickly rushed outside, and I heard her saying to a police officer that there was a Jewish girl in her room. Luckily, the policeman was very much in demand. He addressed her sternly, telling her to return to the room at once and to take care of her belongings as there was a lot of stealing going on.

She had no alternative but to come back to the room, and I gave her an antagonistic stare. In desperation, I began to sing, hoping to appear unconcerned. She did not join in.

Under normal circumstances, I would have asked her if she thought I was Jewish because I had such nice hair.

But now, I began to call her rude names and asked if she was, by any chance, Jewish herself. On that note, she gathered her belongings and hurriedly left the room. My words seemed to have offended her, or perhaps even frightened her.

As soon as she left, I reverted to my previous hair-style. Then I, too, left the room and joined other girls. When I saw my accuser again, I made sure to speak to that policeman, asking for permission to go to the toilet. Seeing that I was not afraid of a policeman, she left me alone, probably believing she had made a big mistake. After all, there were many gentiles who looked more Jewish than I did. Her remarks were a warning to me not to revert to my old hairstyle any more, so as not to give myself away again.

I became very impatient waiting for the train. I honestly believed that the sooner I arrived in Germany, the safer I would be. I joined in with the others when they sang.

19. A Run-In with Zosia

It was November 13, 1942, when we finally left Lublin for Germany. As the train pulled away, I tried to relax by convincing myself that my troubles were over – at least for a little while. When I thought of the precious identity card that I possessed, I even allowed myself to doze off for a little while. However, my previous experiences had taught me not to rejoice too soon, for the identity card was only a piece of paper.

The sense that someone was staring at me awakened me from my light sleep. When I opened my eyes, I almost froze with fear. Sitting directly opposite me was Zosia, a girl who had attended my school. I was absolutely certain that she recognised me, for she was not the type to forget anyone whom she believed had done her wrong. In actuality, it was she who behaved so brutally to my brother and me when we were just children.

A few years before the war, I had gone to the forest with Yechiel and a group of older Jewish children to gather *jagody*, a kind of blueberry, from which our mothers made brandy and baked delicious cakes. We somehow got separated from the group in the dense forest and were left alone not knowing our way out. Since the older girls kept our food and drinks, we were left with only the *jagody* to eat and were crying for help.

When Zosia met us, she refused to tell us how to find our way and insisted we hand over our *jagody*. We held on to the fruit which took us hours to pick and while she struggled to take them away from us, the *jagody* spilled on the ground. We, in turn, emptied her basket of berries, and she had to return home without any *jagody* as well. We did not know why she had done this, but Yechiel and I cried all the way home.

And now this wicked Zosia was going to take her revenge on me. 'I like your beautiful clothes. You look very nice in disguise,' she said to me. 'Remember Majdan Forest and the day you and your horrible brother spilled all my beautiful *jagody* all over the ground?'

I was too frightened to tell her that it was she who had started the fight and kept silent.

'I am freezing,' she said pointedly.

'So am I,' I answered. What she said next sent a shiver through my spine.

'Give me your fur-lined coat, or I will tell the police officer that you are a *Żydówka*,' she said, loud enough for everyone to hear.

My fear left me suddenly and completely, and a new strength entered my body. When I saw what Zosia was trying to do, I was filled with hatred. For the use of my coat, she was prepared to let me die. She was not even a German! She was only a Polish slave being taken to Germany for forced labour.

I was quite prepared to die, though not without a big fight and punishment for that horrible girl. I decided at first to appear indifferent, to divert attention from me.

That was impossible, however; Zosia was causing such a great commotion that all eyes were upon me. It would have been unnatural for me to be indifferent. With all eyes staring accusingly at me, I felt as if I were a wild animal out of its habitat, not a peace-loving girl who wanted one thing – a chance to live. I decided that if I had to die I would take that wicked girl along with me.

I looked Zosia straight in her eyes and announced, 'You are a *warjatka*, a crazy girl.'

'Did I hear the word *Żydówka*?' asked a guard in perfect Polish, only just realising what he had overheard.

The guard must have been a Pole in German uniform or a German born in Poland. It made absolutely no difference. His eyes lit up as if someone had told him that he had just won a million *złotys*, and he took hold of my hand to make sure I would not escape. What a fool he must have been not to have realised that this was quite impossible for me then. Escape was the last thing I had on my mind now. I was going to fight that girl before I died. And, I decided, if I did die, then she would die with me.

I expected the policeman to shoot me right there in front of all the others, which would have greatly satisfied Zosia. I failed to understand why he did not carry out the execution. I gave him the nicest smile, which surprised him, and I spat at Zosia, calling her *warjatka* again. She suddenly appeared greatly agitated and very surprised at my courage – something she could not have visualised earlier, especially coming from a Jewish girl. All of a sudden, I felt like Samson, and I honestly believed at that time that I could fight the whole world

I reassured myself that I was armed with a valid identity card. Only the policeman in Zamość knew how I had obtained it. It was highly unlikely that any of the officers would contact the headquarters in Zamość to inquire about me. They had much more important matters with which to deal. And it was just Zosia's word against mine.

I stood up and began to use the most profane expressions, calling Zosia every degrading name I could bring to mind. As I stared at her, I suddenly realised that she had dark hair and dark eyes. In contrast, I had such light hair that my classmates used to tease me about being an albino. The thought of Zosia looking more Jewish than I gave me encouragement, and I felt that my prayers were being answered.

The guard held me tightly until our next stop but did not beat me. I failed to comprehend why he did not hit me, remembering quite well how cruel the soldiers had been to the people in my town. I decided that I could not have appeared Jewish to him, not with my blond hair and my lack of fear. For who ever heard of a Jewish girl not to show any fear when arrested? This must have greatly surprised him – and wicked Zosia too.

When the train stopped, the police officer led us into the Gestapo headquarters. I smiled broadly and greeted the officers with a cheery good morning.

I asked the black-uniformed brutes, in Polish of course, for a drink of water. My request was refused, so I sat down on a chair and kept smiling at the Gestapo men. A neutral observer would have believed that I had come for a job interview, not to be interrogated. I kept my head high and tried to appear very confident, not at all like a girl who thinks she is going to be killed any minute. I could see they were not quite sure I was Jewish. I saw them talking to each other quietly, and their faces were skeptical. This bolstered my confidence.

'*Was ist dein Name, Mädchen,*' asked a soldier, speaking German. 'What is your name, girl?'

I did not answer and just carried on smiling at all of them, pretending not to have understood the question asked in German.

The guard from the train sat down on a chair next to me and asked me what I had to say about Zosia's accusation. Not showing that I was in the least bit concerned, I gathered all the strength I still had in me, thinking that this was the last time I would need it.

I gave Zosia an antagonistic look. 'She must be crazy,' I retorted. 'Either that or she is Jewish herself. She told me on the train that if I didn't give her my coat, she would tell you that I was Jewish, that *warjatka.*'

The inquisitor turned to my informer with a mean look on his face. I realised, of course, how lucky I was that Zosia failed to inform them that she knew me.

'Is that true?' the officer asked Zosia.

She became very pale. She suddenly seemed too frightened to answer and maybe even sorry that she had started this business. There was no going back, of course. Never for a moment had she imagined that this interrogation would take place. She must have believed that as soon as she told them I was Jewish, they would shoot me. Then she would be able to get my coat as well as take revenge for her beautiful *jagody*.

My eyes were now burning, and I did not take them off Zosia. I could see that the terror was growing in her by the minute. I was already prepared for the worst, she was not. She had everything to live for, I had nothing left to lose. She did not possess my courage – courage which bad experience had taught me. I was at a better advantage by the minute.

The atmosphere in the Gestapo room was very tense. They were all watching me and Zosia; I appeared very relaxed and Zosia more nervous all the time. The Germans began talking among themselves, ignoring us for a while. I was, of course, quite fearful about what would come next as I was afraid that my death sentence would soon be announced. This did not, however, happen so quickly.

The interrogating soldier now wanted to know if I could recite the daily prayer that all Christian children had to recite before lessons began. It had been customary for us Jewish pupils to stand by silently while the others recited their prayer, and having a good memory, I repeated it to the soldier verbatim. I answered all the questions about the Catholic religion, and they seemed satisfied with my knowledge of it.

They had not finished with me yet, but the longer the interrogations took, the more hopeful I became. They seemed to be hesitating, and that suited me. Time was on my side. They all went into another room for a small conference. When they returned, they asked me to sing several songs, including the Polish national anthem.

'*Jeszcze Polska nie zginęła, kiedy my żyjemy,*' I sang. 'Poland has not perished yet, as long as we are still alive.' I reminded my interrogator that Poland had already perished.

He translated my comment, which seemed to please them all. They all began to laugh aloud, while I put on a dejected face.

'My country has vanished along with my soldier cousins,' I added, appearing to be very cross with them for taking away our country.

They all seemed to admire me – a courageous, outspoken Polish girl who was not afraid to speak her mind in front of the Gestapo.

All through my interrogation, I could hear the sound of people being tortured with dogs, and my heart went out to them. Their agonising screams only made me more determined not to suffer the same fate. I had to extricate myself from this predicament, and I began to curse Zosia.

I addressed her angrily. 'I heard that it is very cold in Germany. You're not going to get my nice warm coat, not now and not in Germany, you wicked crazy girl! I hope you never get there. I hope they throw you to the dogs.'

To my relief, the beastly tormentors started accusing Zosia of being Jewish. I could see she regretted having betrayed me, but it was already too late. She could not take her words back.

The undecided Gestapo torturers took us into an adjoining room where the commanding officer was sitting comfortably. The fat beast, for that is what he looked like, began to look me up and down. He was drunk and not sure that I was Jewish; I knew that this was a good sign. I smiled at him innocently, but suddenly, he announced my death sentence by saying that even if they made a mistake, and I turned out not to be Jewish, then there would be one less Polish worm.

'Take her to the dogs at once!' he said.

I had to think fast, before it was too late.

I stood up proudly and fearlessly. I knew that they did not expect me to have understood what they were saying if I were really Polish and not Jewish. To make doubly certain they believed me, I complained to the Polish-speaking officer that I was very hungry and thirsty and asked him when they were going to give me something to eat.

'You are not going to get anything here,' he said in a very unfriendly tone.

'Are you going to starve me?' I asked him and began to cry bitterly.

That Polish-speaking officer translated what I was saying to the others who began to make fun of me.

'Take her away to the dogs!' the one in charge repeated in German.

But none of them touched me. Something kept them away from me.

'What are you waiting for?' asked the leader.

I was not going to wait longer, for I had not even a minute left. I still pretended not to understand German, as Yiddish is so similar to German, it may have given me away, and went straight over to Zosia. I scratched her

148

face as hard as I could with my long, dirty nails until blood began dripping down her cheeks and onto her nice clean clothes.

'This is my coat, and I need it, and I will kill you for trying to take it away from me, you selfish girl!' I screamed.

There was now such a lot of hate in me that I probably could have killed her.

'Stop fighting!' the commanding officer shouted. He then turned to the soldier who had brought me in and berated him sternly. 'I thought you were quite certain that she was Jewish. She didn't understand a word I said. Don't disturb me again, and don't waste my time any more.'

He poured some whisky into a glass and drank it quickly, appearing to become more drunk with each swallow. That suited me quite well. He could not think clearly any more, while my mind became more and more clear. Fearlessly, I kept on staring at him. He, in turn, observed me with disbelief.

I sat down and then got up again without permission. Gathering all my courage, I went over to him and indicated that I wanted a drink from his bottle, but he pushed me away just with his bare hands. I gave him an extra-nice smile and sat down and repeated my request for a drink of water, which, of course, I did not get. He did not understand a single Polish word.

In an apparent rage, he began to shout, 'She looks less like a Jewess than the one who denounced her.'

The soldier looked frightened and apologised for wasting his time.

'Let her go at once!' said the officer. 'Question the

other one.' He turned towards Zosia, who only a short while before had basked in the glory of an informer. 'She looks very Jewish to me,' he repeated.

'*Mach dass du fort kommst*!' he shouted at me. 'Get out of here!'

I could not leave quickly enough but pretended I did not understand him. I just continued watching him drink. It made him very cross, and he told the officer to take me back to the station and never to waste his time again.

Breathing a silent sigh of relief, I left the Gestapo headquarters with a different police officer. He accompanied me to the station to await the next train.

Zosia never came back, and I could well imagine what happened to her.

BOOK THREE
Amid the Enemy

20. Alias Stefania

The interrogation had taken its toll on me, and I sat on a bench to give myself a much needed rest. 'Goodbye, Mala Szorer,' I said to myself. 'Now I am Stefania Iwkiewicz.' Another good Christian name, just like Marysia had been. It occurred to me, however, that the name Iwkiewicz was Ukrainian, and I was claiming to be Polish. I hoped the Germans would not discover that mistake. I wondered if Zosia had been killed. She would have deserved it, but that thought did not make me happy. Now that the danger had passed and I was more myself, I pitied that foolish girl.

Everyone in the station was staring at me with amazement, for I had entered the room with a German police officer. Though the curiosity on their faces was plain, they seemed afraid to question me. One girl, however, approached me and offered to share her sandwiches.

'Thanks, but I have my own,' I told her.

'Why did you enter with the police officer?' she suddenly blurted out.

'This is a secret between us,' I said.

She looked at me curiously but said no more. I allowed myself a little smile and left her guessing.

I sat next to another girl who became increasingly curious about what happened.

'Don't tell anyone I told you,' I said. 'I tried to escape and go back home.'

'How foolish of you!' she said. 'You never would have made it.'

'I would not,' I agreed. 'I was foolish, but I hated leaving my country to go to a strange place. I thought they might treat us very badly there or even starve us.'

'We will all have to endure it together,' she comforted me. 'And don't ever try to escape again.'

'I won't,' I assured her.

She then told everybody what I had attempted to do, adding that I had lost my shoes in my flight. Her need to inform the others about me suited me well.

We waited in the bitter cold for the train. It was not much warmer inside, for our transportation was not a proper train but an unheated cattle car. Sitting on the hard floor, I covered my feet with my long coat, trying to warm up and relax. Feeling safe with my new identity card, I dozed off.

I awoke to find a boy heading in my direction. Was he also going to demand my coat? I wondered. I knew quite well that a typical boy would not want to start a conversation with a girl who was dressed as peculiarly as I was. He did not seem to notice how odd I looked and kept approaching. He told me that he was a doctor's son and had seen my injured thumb. (My thumb had become a bit mangled during my fight with Zosia.) He said it would require immediate attention, or else it would become septic.

'Here, have this,' he said, handing me a bit of antiseptic zinc ointment. 'What happened to it?'

'I tripped while running,' I lied.

'I'm not at all surprised you did, dressed in that long coat and those oversized socks. Don't you have anything else of your own?'

'My stepmother didn't allow me to take any of my belongings with me,' I explained. 'She despised me because I told my father that she wasn't as nice as my real mother used to be.'

'Where was your father when you left?'

'He was tending his horses,' I lied. 'Since he remarried, they have become more important to him than I am.'

'Well, I will just have to look after you,' he said kindly. But I knew that I could look after myself better than anyone else could, and I hoped that we would be assigned to different towns, which we were.

A girl sitting directly across from me overheard our conversation and tried her best to console me. 'You have your whole life in front of you,' she said. 'By the time you get back from Germany you will be big enough to fend for yourself. Perhaps you will meet a nice boy and get married.'

The girl offered me an extra bandage and a sandwich of bread and butter. Her food, generosity and warmth refreshed and comforted me. I desperately needed some-one to cheer me up after my ordeal, and she sounded so sympathetic.

'Did you say your name was Stefania?' she asked. 'You're not by any chance from Tarnogród, are you? I have a distant relative by that name. She lives there.'

My heart skipped a beat. 'No,' I said. 'I'm not from

Tarnogród. I have never heard of Tarnogród. I come from Pikule, near Janów. What's that Stefania's surname?'

'To be honest, I don't remember,' she replied. 'We don't keep in touch with them. We live in Łukowa.'

The information that she lived in Łukowa did not sit well with me. That town was only two hours away from Tarnogród by horse and cart. How glad I was to hear that she did not keep in touch with her relatives. I realised that I had again had a narrow escape, and I said a special prayer of thanks.

I closed my eyes to avoid further conversation, and the girl went to look for other company. Somehow, I would have to do something to avoid encountering her again. I decided to move to a different part of the train and start a conversation with someone else. I was still worried that my name might be called out or that I would be assigned to the same town as the other girl. She might remember that her relative's name was Iwkiewicz.

From afar, I saw a girl, sitting alone, so I joined her. She seemed friendly enough and introduced herself as Marysia.

'I wish we could have some comfortable seats,' she said as I sat down beside her. 'I'm exhausted.'

'So am I,' I told her. 'But there is a war on now, and we all have to bear our share of the burden. They'll probably let us rest when we get to Germany.'

'I hope we get there soon. I'm freezing,' she said.

'I would gladly give you some clothes, but I only have one spare sweater,' I told her. I arranged my long coat so that its hem covered her feet. 'Here, this might help.'

My coat had fallen open when I readjusted it, making my nightgown visible.

'Why are you wearing a nightgown?' she asked.

'It only looks like a nightgown,' I said. 'It's really a funny dress that my stepmother made for me.'

'My stepmother is very nice, and I love her,' she said.

We now had a lot in common and something to talk about. I needed company, and here was someone to whom I could pour out my heart, even if it was only to complain about my wicked stepmother.

I left the bulk of the conversation up to Marysia, who chattered away. She did not seem too bright, and I hoped that we would be assigned to the same town where we could become friends. I knew that the more intelligent the people around me were, the more likely they would eventually notice that I was different. If I were forced to go to church, I would not know how to sing their hymns. Marysia, though, knew even less than I did. Next to hers, my ignorance would not be so remarkable.

I knew that I had to have more items of clothing so that my future employer should not become too suspicious.

'Can you do me a favour?' I asked Marysia. 'Ask the others if they've got any spare clothes. I'll share them with you.'

Obediently, Marysia got up and approached several girls. She returned a few minutes later with a few sweaters and three skirts. Good luck was with me once again. I now had clothes and a good friend. It was as if *Hashem* had sent Marysia to me, a nice girl whom I could sincerely like.

The new police officer did not bother us during the journey. He may have spoken our language, but he was a German and could not be bothered with a few 'Polish worms'. If only my parents could see me now, I thought. They would be proud that the lessons they had taught me were helping me to survive.

'You seem very quiet,' said Marysia. 'Don't you want to talk to me?'

'I'll tell you what,' I said. 'You talk, and I'll listen.'

As she spoke, I pictured my family, and a burning desire to return to Tarnogród overcame me. I imagined them standing on the doorstep and inviting me in. I would tell them what I, still a teenager, had managed to do so far, and I knew they would smile at me with admiration and love.

An unbidden memory suddenly flashed into my mind's eye. I remembered the time my mother had asked me to take my younger sisters out to play. Instead of obeying, I had replied that I had to go to my friend's house and memorise a poem. Now, on the train full of sad-looking youths and stone-faced police, I asked my family for their forgiveness and said goodbye as I never had before.

'Please forgive me, all of you, for all my wrongdoing,' I said silently. 'You were the best family anyone could have hoped to have. Thank you, dear mother, for looking after me when I was young. Thank you for the hot meals you cooked for me. Thank you for the lovely dresses you sewed for me. How silly I was to have complained about them. You did your best, mother dear. You stayed up late at night to do all the sewing for me and my sisters. I shall never forget you, for now I realise that you were the best mother in the whole world. If only you could see how much I miss you now.

'Darling father, I understand only now how you used to risk your life to go out to the surrounding villages to make a living. You left very early every morning and came home late at night with your beard frozen solid in winter time. I was too young and foolish to appreciate it then. To you, dear father, I want to say thank you. You were the best father anyone could have had.

'Thank you, dearest Balla, for helping to look after me when I was young. Thank you for the nice dresses you sent me from Warsaw. You always answered my letters. Through your letters and the *Sabina* magazines you sent, I learned about the big city; I almost knew what Warsaw looked like.

'I'm sorry, Yechiel, for all the fights we had. I was just a child then, but I have grown up since then. If only you were here, I would always give in to you. I would never be selfish again.

'How I miss you, sweet Esther, Kresele and Surele, my sweet little sisters. May *Hashem* help you rest in peace, all of you. I shall love you forever and keep you engraved in my memory as long as I shall live.'

Soon, the train came to a halt and ended my meditation. We had reached the town of Dessau, where we received some refreshments. German civilians and soldiers, talking to each other, filled the station. They did not bother speaking to us, Polish slaves that we were. Even if they had, no one would have understood them.

No one, that is, except me. I understood almost everything they were saying, but I could never reveal that. I kept quiet like the rest.

We were ordered to strip and stand in front of some Nazis. I tried desperately to cover myself with my scarf, but it was torn away from me. I felt humiliated by their snickers and leers, and so did the others. We all looked subdued. After a while, we were told to put our clothes back on and to board the train for our next destination.

Marysia was now holding my arm, saying she was not sure what awaited us in that strange country and that we would have to stick together. 'How are we going to speak to our employers?' she asked. 'I don't understand a word of German, do you?'

'No, not one word,' I said. 'But I'll be happy to be your friend. I hope we'll be assigned to the same area, but you're older and can probably cook well. You'll probably be assigned to a large rich household. I can only clean.'

'If they put us in the same household, I'd teach you how to cook,' said Marysia.

'It's not up to us,' I reminded her. 'Let's wait and see.' I did not really want to handle *trief* food, especially for the Germans. I also did not like feeding them.

We arrived in Dresden and were taken to a quarantine building. There we were disinfected, before travelling on to a small town near Leipzig in Saxony. We alighted and were taken to the Labour Exchange. The Nazis formed us into arbitrary groups, and mine was assigned to work in a chocolate factory. There were so many in the group that I was afraid I would run into someone who knew me and would give me away. I knew that it was also necessary for me to get away from that group because most of them had seen me with the Gestapo. Any of them might reveal that information, and the Germans would eventually wonder about it. Thus, as we were marched through the streets of the town, I memorised the route and, after a few minutes, slipped away from the group.

I retraced my steps and entered the Labour Exchange without anyone noticing me. The crowd of new arrivals was even bigger than the one I had deserted. Frightened again, I picked my way carefully through the crowd, trying to appear unconcerned.

I went to the bathroom and stayed there for quite a long time, until I could hear no more voices. When I came out, the only ones left in the room were two officers, Malach and I.

'Why didn't we see you before?' one officer suddenly asked.

I pretended that I did not understand his question and heard him say to his partner that there was no point in detaining me. Someone could do with a girl like me, he said.

He picked up the telephone, and I could hear him speaking to someone.

'Herr Perlmutt? You said you needed a girl for scrubbing and cleaning at the guest house. We have here a very silly, odd-looking girl. If you would care to come over to have a look for yourself, you are welcome to take her with you.' He paused for a moment before continuing. 'I am warning you that I think she is only good for scrubbing.'

I hoped that Herr Perlmutt would turn out to be a friendly man. I did not really care about the type of work I was going to do. As long as I got food and a soft bed in return for my labour, I would feel satisfied. I longed to belong to someone; it did not really matter that I was going to be a mere scrub girl. I used to be quite good at housework at home, and maybe I even enjoyed doing it. I was going to surprise them with how well such a primitive-looking girl could really clean.

Exhausted from so much worrying, I sat and awaited my future boss, hoping he would not be as cruel as the young soldiers in Poland. Before long, a very plump gentleman arrived. He looked at my attire with amazement and announced, 'Yes, she is good enough for scrubbing,' and with this remark, he signalled me to follow him.

It seemed a very long walk to his house, since I still had only socks on my feet and sleet had begun to fall. At the entrance to the house, Herr Perlmutt indicated that I should wait. He called for someone to bring out some slippers before I entered his guest house. I put on the wooden clogs and felt thrilled with the good fortune of having shoes on my feet, even if they were too big for me. They were not even suitable for going outside, but they were better than mere stockings, and I looked a little less preposterous.

Eventually, I was called to the kitchen, which was fairly large and very tidy. I waited for quite a few minutes before a very chubby Frau Perlmutt appeared. I observed her closely and was pleased to see that she seemed very friendly. There was no hatred in her eyes at confronting a Polish girl; they seemed to be filled with pity for such a peculiar-looking young girl. I was self-conscious and hoped she would not think I dressed like this by choice.

Frau Perlmutt managed to convey that her abode was a combined hotel and restaurant. She signalled to me to follow her into the cellar utility room in which she stored cleaning materials. As expected, my main task would be cleaning. No language was needed to explain that, I realised to my delight.

During the first few days of my stay there, Frau Perlmutt managed to explain to me exactly what my duties would be. She was more than surprised that although she could not communicate with me, I somehow managed to fulfil my duties to her satisfaction. Only then did I realise that not all Germans hated those who were not of their own kind, for here was a lady who seemed to like me from the very start. I was not really surprised because I worked twice as hard as the German girls, who completely ignored me.

Hard work did not frighten me, for I was accustomed to it since childhood. I was grateful to be occupied at last, something I had longed for during my time in the forests. I began to count my blessings and considered myself very lucky indeed. My prayers had been temporarily answered.

My only immediate problems were getting used to my new self-given name and pretending that I did not understand German. Of course, I understood it quite well. Later, the 'language problem' led to some amusing incidents. Once, for example, the Perlmutts asked me to bring them a *korb*, a basket; I knew she wanted to serve bread in it, but I purposely asked the cook for a *kork*, a cork. However, Frau Perlmutt was a patient woman.

She was also very kind, and before long she asked the neighbours whether they could spare some clothing for me. She also bought me some underwear and a pair of much-needed shoes. I was so grateful that Frau Perlmutt was prompted to say, '*Der Weihnachtsmann wird schon die andere Sachen bringen.* Father Christmas will bring the other things you need.'

I let on that I understood some of what she said. It was hard to resist the urge to show that I understood their language and was not so stupid as they imagined me to be. I did not think she would become suspicious, for I could have picked up a few words of German since the occupation of Poland. However, Frau Perlmutt was very surprised, so I would have to be careful.

On Christmas Eve, the Perlmutts took me to church, the only time I ever went with them. I received many items of clothes as Christmas presents from them, some of which were new and some had been donated by their friends. I could see that it was important to the Perl-mutts that I looked presentable. Herr and Frau Perlmutt also gave me other presents and a card, a gesture that surprised me and a kindness I did not expect of Ger-mans. They certainly did not see me as a Polish worm. Most likely, they understood how it felt to be uprooted at such a young age, especially at the time of year when families celebrated Christmas together.

The workers were not as friendly as the Perlmutts. None of them even spared me a smile. Because I did not speak their language, they adopted an air of arrogance and superiority over me. They also treated me to some petty meanness. They would not, for instance, allow me to sit at their table during meals. Instead, they forced me to take my meals with an abnormal boy called Manfred. His only duty was to wash the cutlery as he was not capable of doing anything else. I was given a room in the maidservants' quarters in the attic, together with the others, but they did not bother with me though their rooms were near mine. This was for the best as I might have been tempted to show them that I understood German. That would have made them suspicious from the start, not only later on as it turned out. Therefore, I did not mind too much when they ignored me. Still, lonely as I was, I would have appreciated a little smile.

As simple as it was, I immediately fell in love with my room. It was not more than a cell with a stone floor, but it seemed like a palace to me. I slept very soundly those first weeks.

One night, however, I awoke to the sound of sirens. Foreign planes had appeared over German skies, but in my half-conscious state, I imagined that I was still in Tarnogród. I jumped out of bed at once, grabbed my fur-lined coat and rushed downstairs to the dining room. It was filled with soldiers who were calmly eating and drinking. Without thinking, I asked in Yiddish, '*Wus is du gevehn*? What has happened here?' Not understanding what I had said, Herr Perlmutt came over to me and pushed me out of the room, shouting, '*Du dummes Sch-wein! Raus hier!* You silly pig! Get out of here.'

Flabbergasted, I went back to my room. By then I was wide awake and realised I must have put Herr Perlmutt to shame in front of all his customers. I was thankful that no one had noticed that I spoke in Yiddish. They had obviously not heard it before and must have believed that I had spoken pure Polish. I counted myself lucky and hoped no one would ever repeat my words to people who would know better and report me to the authorities.

It was quite easy for me to pretend I was a Christian girl; it was not so easy to eat the *treif* food, and I asked *Hashem* for guidance. At the beginning I tried to adhere, as far as possible, to Jewish dietary laws. I ate only dairy and left the meat and the hard cheese on my plate. I did not realise the consequences of my actions. The other workers seemed surprised by my eating habits and whispered among themselves, but I did not make much of it.

Before I went to sleep one night, I washed my black and white apron and stockings. Exhausted as always, I fell asleep immediately. All of a sudden, my mother opened my door. The landing was lit up, and I could distinctly see all the items of clothing that I had hung on the washing line before I bolted the door. My mother came right up to my bed and said, 'Dear child, downstairs there is a whole conversation going on about you. They are discussing your strange eating habits. If you do not eat everything they give you, you will not survive.'

Although I was sleeping, I remembered that she was no longer alive. I woke up with a sudden quiver and went to try the door. I found it to be as securely locked and bolted as it had been when I went to sleep. I made such a commotion checking the door that Herr Perlmutt came up to investigate. Not wanting to show him that I understood German, I did not answer. I went back to sleep, but I clearly remembered my mother's advice the next morning. I could hardly believe that my mother had come to warn me. She was still able to help me, even now that she was dead.

21. Letters from Home

A short while after my dream, I overheard the staff talking about me. They said that it was most peculiar for a young girl not to receive any mail from her parents, especially when she was so far away from home. One girl suggested I might have escaped from somewhere.

'Maybe that's the reason she works so hard,' she said. 'So that the Perlmutts never find cause for complaint. And if she is a Catholic, as she claims to be, why doesn't she ever pray or wear the rosary? And why does she look frightened every time a high-ranking officer enters the hotel?' they asked.

I resolved to be more careful in the future and less obedient. The next time Frau Perlmutt entered my room, I picked up my black blanket and indicated that I did not like it. It was cold at night, and I wanted an eiderdown.

'It looks like she is used to something better,' said Herr Perlmutt, who was standing next to his wife.

In the evening, I found my blanket gone, an eiderdown in its place.

I began to behave as if I were one of them now. I was just a little less obedient than before but still a very good worker. The next step in my campaign was to show that leftovers displeased me. From then on, I received only fresh portions of food. My plan worked well, and they even began to show respect for me.

There was still the matter of mail with which I had to deal. If I were to convince my workmates that their suspicions were groundless, I would have to figure out a way to receive mail from 'home'. I lay awake, worrying about my predicament. Suddenly, I remembered a Polish family whose address I knew by heart. The mother, whose name happened to be Stefania, had been taken to Oswiecim-Auschwitz because she belonged to the Polish Intelligentsia. I planned to write to that family and convince the poor father that I was his wife.

It was quite out of my nature to cause harm to innocent people, so I pondered for a while whether it was right or wrong to give them false hope. However, my life depended on it, and I decided to carry out my plan. Without further ado, I put pen to paper:

Dear Maciek,

You are probably wondering why my handwriting is different from the one you know so well. This is because I injured my right thumb on the train that was taking me to Germany. As a result, I am now compelled to write with my left hand. Please also forgive my poor style in writing. I am still too weak from the initial shock of my injury.

Please don't worry about me, dear, because it is now healing quite nicely. I am concerned about all of you and hope you are managing well. How I long to see all of you, but I doubt if that will be possible while the war lasts. I sincerely trust that everyone at home is keeping well and that you have enough to eat. How are the children doing at school? I am working in a hotel as a maidservant, and I have become an expert at making beds, cleaning and washing dishes. Every day, we have about three hundred people, mainly soldiers, for dinner. I am the only dishwasher. I am quite proud of myself as I can see that the Perlmutts are quite satisfied with me. I have the right job. I eat well, and I am getting fatter and fatter all the time. I hardly need any meat when I finish the thick pea soups. But as you know, I don't like meat very much. Please write often, all of you, as I am lonely here.

Your loving Stefania

I hesitated a little before mailing my letter and wondered what had happened to me. I had been such an honest girl. Now, here I was, deceiving a whole family! I consoled myself with the thought that I never actually said I was Maciek's wife.

It did not take very long before I had my first reply from my 'family'. The letter, as were all the others, was written with great longing for a quick reunion. The children, who must have been delighted that their mother was alive, also started to write. They were very careful about what they wrote to me and did not question me about how I had managed to escape. I presume that they kept their 'mother's' escape a secret from all their friends, for fear of her being betrayed and arrested again. Every time I wrote a letter to that family, trepidation filled my heart, but I could not think of anything else to do. While it brought this unfortunate family false hope, it brought me my life. For that reason, it was worth lying. But I prayed that *Hashem* would forgive me for my sins.

Being fond of letter writing, I wrote often and always received speedy replies. For a while, this was quite normal procedure, until one fateful day it almost blew up in my face. The story was as follows.

Among the staff of the hotel were two German sisters. They had been born in Danzig, Poland, but miraculously knew only a handful of Polish words. One day, when I was reading a letter from my newly acquired daughter, the older of the two sisters, Charlotte, caught sight of the opening line which read, '*Kochana Mama*, Dearest Mother.'

'What nonsense is this, Stefania?' she exclaimed. 'How can you be a mother at your age?'

Controlling my fear, I told her, in the rudest way possible, that she had no right to look at my letters. I also told her that she had mistakenly read *Mama* instead of *Manio*, which is maid. In reality, the Polish word for maid is *służąca*, but I counted on her not knowing that. I then ran upstairs, pretending to be extremely cross with her intrusion into my privacy. I slammed the door to my room behind me and locked it securely. Tearing the letter into tiny little shreds, I hid the pieces under the floorboards, fearful that someone would search my room in my absence and discover them.

The next time I ventured outside, I disposed of the evidence in a public dustbin, far away from the hotel. There was nothing else to do except hope that the family would not write to me again. My prayers were answered. Not receiving any more letters from me, my 'husband' must have decided that his wife had either assumed a different identity or been arrested and it was not safe to write to her again. That suited me well. For her part, Charlotte did not mention the letter again.

After that incident, I made it my business to be the only one to pick up all the mail, in case another letter arrived for me. My luck was still with me, for I received no more letters from my 'children'. However, I knew I still had to receive letters from Poland; this was crucial for my survival. I had many sleepless nights, pondering a move that would not arouse further suspicions.

One night, when sleep proved elusive, I had a brain-wave. I devised a new plan and hoped it would work better than the first. This time, I would have to take the risk of asking for help.

I was lucky to have made several friends among the Polish workers in town. It had been easy to make them like me; all I had to do was not steal their boyfriends as some other girls did and not argue with them. A few of them were illiterate, so I wrote their letters home for them.

We had got into the custom of meeting in a park on Sundays. We could safely sit around and complain about our employers, for Germans did not go to that park. They were not very keen to mix with our 'inferior' race. That suited us well. The park belonged to us alone, and we felt as if we were back in Poland while we were there.

The next time I met my Polish friends in the park, I put my plan into action. I succeeded in convincing them that I would become a writer when I was older. I would then tell the whole world how much we had suffered in Germany. My book would be filled with the particulars of how we had been separated from our families. I told them that it was my intention that the world should know about us. They would all be famous when Poland was liberated.

They were so caught up in my fantasy of fame and freedom, they began to sing the Polish anthem. I joined right in, singing loudly, clapping my hands. '*Jeszcze Polska nie zginęła, kiedy my żyjemy*, Poland has not yet perished as long as we live.' Everyone smiled at me, and I smiled in return. It was quite genuine; those were lovely girls and boys.

'We have been taken away from our parents against our will,' I said to my friends, 'but in order to record how we suffered, I must practise my writing. I am only a young girl, after all, whose education was interrupted. My own family is not good at letter-writing. Would you all let me have some addresses of your friends and relations so that I may write to them? I need lots of practice.'

There was a long silence, and I could hear much whispering. Then, some of them began to mock me, saying they would also write a book one day. I thought I would have to scrap my plan, until a boy named Jurek suddenly announced, 'Why should she write the book when she is the youngest? Let someone older and more mature volunteer, and we shall all give our consent.'

They had begun to take me seriously!

We waited for a while, but no one else volunteered, and they left it to me to write a book. Right then, I had no notion of doing that. All I wanted at the time were many addresses, even if it meant deceiving my friends.

'Are you sure that you're not working for the Germans?' one asked suddenly and suspiciously.

'How is it that you seem to understand more German than we do?' asked another.

'I don't,' I lied. 'I only pretend to understand. I am a very good pretender!' And I laughed heartily.

'Do it, Stefin, dear,' a girl named Janina said. 'We shall all buy your book one day.'

A week later, I received many addresses in Poland and also Germany and Austria, where some of their friends were doing forced labour. When I took those addresses home, I felt as if I had become very rich. They were very precious to me as they were crucial to my survival. I wrote letters in my room, pad propped against my knees, after a hard day's work. My letters were carefully worded. I dared not disclose more than the information that I did not receive mail from home and I was, therefore, lonely and in need of correspondence.

It took quite a while before I received any replies, so each time the mail came, I had to pretend to be hysterical when there was no post for me. On one occasion, I pushed away my breakfast and cried bitterly with false tears. Frau Perlmutt clucked her tongue and remarked, 'Something dreadful must have occurred at her home. Perhaps there was a death in her family.'

At long last, I received a letter from a girl called Maryla Kobylarz. She was working in Vienna, she wrote, and her sister Zosia Flamer worked in Magdenburg, Germany. If I wanted, I could also correspond with Zosia. It puzzled me how two sisters could have different surnames. I pondered a long time over this discrepancy and came to the conclusion that they must have been Jewish and, like me, had changed their names to survive. I then wrote to Zosia, and within a short time, I received her letter. She informed me that she and her sister Maryla came from Pysznica.

The information stunned me. Pysznica was a small town near Nisko, where my grandmother had been living. I wrote back to tell her that my grandmother married a man called M. B. (Moshe Brand) and that they also lived in Pysznica. I next told Zosia that I came from Tarnogród and that my oldest sister B. (Balla) lived with our grandmother, who paid for her to learn first-class dressmaking near Pysznica, in a town called Nisko.

After an exchange of a few letters, Maryla, Zosia and I began to realise that we were, in fact, related. Their grandfather was my grandmother's second husband. I became very excited and eagerly awaited the time when we could meet. Unfortunately, to date, my dream has not yet been realised although, many years later, I learned that they moved to New York after the war. I do not know their married names or where they now live. I am still hoping to make contact with them one day and perhaps they will contact me, if they read this book.

22. Aroused Suspicions

One evening in early 1943, Frau Perlmutt asked me to stay downstairs after work as she wanted to have a confidential chat with me. I feared the worst: somehow she had discovered that I was Jewish.

Was I going to die, after all? Perhaps my luck had run out. Frau Perlmutt, however, looked as friendly as ever and rather concerned.

'Sit down, Stefin dear,' she said. 'You don't have to stand.'

Great anxiety engulfed me, but I did not show any hint of fear. I smiled as I always did when she spoke to me, and I sat down.

Frau Perlmutt seemed to find it difficult to begin the conversation with me, especially since she had to repeat everything a number of times and use sign language, to accommodate my supposed ignorance of the German language.

'You must be very tired,' she began. 'It is rather late.'

'I am. I was just going to go to sleep when you called me. Did I do anything wrong today, Frau Perlmutt?'

'Oh, no,' she answered. 'You always carry out your duties satisfactorily. I would just like to tell you what some Germans did to the Jewish people in Leipzig, my home town. They arrested all of them and took them to a concentration camp, where most of them perished.'

While I was happy to hear that there were still some Jewish people alive, I realised that I was being suspected of being Jewish myself. I knew that I had to appear indifferent, as if this information did not really concern me. But I also realised that I had only been fooling myself; that I had been foolish to think I would survive in Germany. I should have stayed with Auntie Aniela, where I could have had more chance of survival, but I was trapped now, and it was too late to think about returning to Poland.

An inner voice, bidding me to keep up my courage and not to surrender, calmed the panic coursing through me. The voice also brought me a measure of practical resolve. Though I would not be naive enough to place Frau Perlmutt above suspicion, I remembered that she was very kind. Her little talk might have been a warning to me that I was suspected of being Jewish and should act more carefully.

If Frau Perlmutt expected to get any reply from me, she was greatly mistaken. I smiled at my boss as if waiting for her to tell me something new. I yawned a few times and stood up.

'Frau Perlmutt, why are you telling me all this?' I asked. 'It doesn't interest me in the least.'

Bidding her a polite good night, I ran upstairs. In the safety of my room, I pondered the significance of Frau Perlmutt's conversation with me. I failed to comprehend why she had suddenly chosen to tell me those things after I had been there for one and a half years. I tried very hard to remember what I had done or said to arouse suspicion.

Everyone had seen me avoiding meat and other non-kosher food; but that could not have been the cause, for I had started eating all the food after my mother appeared in my dream. Charlotte had seen the letter with the '*Kochana Mama*' salutation; but that had been long before Frau Perlmutt's little talk. I concluded that my German was much too good for a Pole; I had 'learned' to speak German too quickly, more quickly than the other Polish workers. Someone, perhaps one of the Polish workers, had suspected me and informed the police. Maybe the police had asked Frau Perlmutt to talk to me to see how I would react.

Oh, why had I not kept up with the pretence just a little longer? It was useless, however, to berate myself. The damage had already been done, and now I had to think of how to rectify my mistakes. I fully realised that this would not be easy, and I asked the Almighty to help me. I quickly said my prayers and began to look for Malach in all directions. I soon found her under the bed, and I was again reassured. I fell asleep knowing that *Hashem* must still be watching over me.

In the following days, I did not forget that the Perlmutts had some doubt about whether I was really a Christian girl. I consoled myself that this knowledge had not gone any further, or I would have been dead by then.

The next Sunday, however, events took another bad turn.

It was compulsory for all foreign workers to report to the police station every Sunday. The Germans kept check on us that way to see if we had escaped or even left the town, which was forbidden to all foreign workers. Normally, those formalities took only a few minutes. Each of us would go into an office, put our signature in a roll book next to our names and leave the police station.

The Sunday after Frau Perlmutt's conversation with me, I went to the station as usual to sign in. There was a new superintendent in charge, but I thought nothing of it and signed in.

I was almost out the door when the superintendent stopped me.

'Just a minute,' he said. 'Don't go yet, Stefania. I want to ask you a few questions first.'

I must have looked concerned, for he said, 'Don't worry, just take a seat. You work in the guest house with the Perlmutts, don't you? They call you Stefin, is that right?'

'Yes,' I said.

He seemed to be waiting for a further response, and I chattered nervously, 'They find it hard to pronounce Stefciu. Stefin – that's a German name, I guess. To tell you the truth, I almost feel German by now, and a lot of people think I am. As you know, I work with German people, and I learned quite a bit of the language. I am very good at learning languages.'

'What other languages can you speak, Stefin?'

'Why, Polish, of course.'

'I was told that you speak that language beautifully.'

'You were told?' I asked. 'My friends told you that I can speak my language well? How come you questioned them about me?'

'I never said I questioned your friends,' he said, imitating my emphasis. 'The people who told me may not be your friends. What other languages can you speak, Stefin?'

'I understand a little bit of Ukrainian because my father spoke that language very well,' I said and immediately regretted babbling on. If he would now ask me my father's or mother's name, he would see me hesitate. I quickly thought of names for them.

'Iwkiewicz is not really a Polish name,' he challenged. 'It's either Russian or Ukrainian. So what are you really, Stefin?'

'I am Polish!' I told him. 'And you should know, sir!'

I was glad he did not ask me the names of my parents.

'Now tell me, Stefin, how many sisters and brothers do you have?'

I got up abruptly and in a very cross manner announced, 'Don't you know what you did to my family in Pikule? You sprayed paraffin on my whole village and burned everything. Everyone was burned alive except for me and another girl.'

I took out my handkerchief and wiped away the tears now pouring down my face. I was glad I could cry; I would appear too upset to answer if he decided to ask the name of the other survivor. I should have known her name! How lucky I was that he never asked me.

The friendly look on his face when I was expecting hostility confused me. I was further bewildered when he asked me to come early next Sunday, at 10:30, when he would be on duty alone.

'Write down your address on this piece of paper before you go,' he said.

This request was also puzzling, because he already knew my address from my identity card. Still, I had no choice and wrote 'Pikule, County Lublin' on a piece of scrap paper he held out to me. I hoped it was right for I had never been to Pikule. I only knew that it was a tiny village and that it probably did not have any street names or numbers. I could feel that he did not believe a word I was telling him, but I failed to understand why he wasted such a long time with me, a mere Polish worm. Finally, my inquisitor announced that I was free to go and even wished me a nice day.

I knew that I would have to search for a way to overcome a new predicament. I could now no longer remember how many times I had had to do that to escape death.

Not having anything else to do, I decided to visit Marysia, who was also free on Sundays. She had married in Germany, and she and her husband worked as housekeepers for a rich German family. Both Marysia and her husband were illiterate, and sometimes I would write letters to Poland for them. They were very grateful for that and always gave me a loaf of bread and some fruit in return.

Together with her husband, we went for a long walk and soon came to the park. We sat down on a bench, and

I could feel right away that there was something going on in my friends' minds.

'My husband wants me to tell you something,' Marysia said. 'You're a very bad mixer, Stefciu dear, and we notice that boys don't really interest you. We can both see that you are very lonely. My husband has a very nice cousin who works in Bitterfeld not far from here, and we think he would be just right for you.' I saw that they were observing me to see what my reaction was.

Looking up, I saw her husband's Ukrainian badge. I must have seen it before, but this was the first time it had any significance to me: Ukrainians were reputed to be almost as bad as Germans. I decided then and there to end our friendship as they might have been the ones who betrayed me to the police.

Marysia forged ahead. 'We are best friends, are we not? And now we could be related, too! Imagine, you could be like a sister-in-law! What do you say to that, Stefciu?'

I felt faint for a minute and then announced that I would love this more than anything else but that I was not ready for marriage yet. 'I still like my freedom, and I want to wait until this war is over. The way Germany is winning on all fronts, it won't take long before they take the whole world, America and England included.'

'I hope you're right. You seem to be well informed,' her husband said, pleased with my predictions. 'Then we'll also have our own country. That's what Germany is promising the Ukrainians. You, Stefciu, could become one of us, our flesh and blood.'

'To tell you the truth, I know a very nice boy in Janów. We write to each other. But let me think it over,' I said.

'Promise?'

'Yes,' I lied. 'Thanks so much for being such genuine friends.'

We joined the usual group of Polish workers, and one of the girls told me I looked as if I had seen a ghost. I could not tell her that it was not a ghost that was worrying me, but the thought that I had to give an answer to Marysia. It tormented me, for my answer was obviously going to be 'no'. I did not know how she and her husband would react; I only knew that if they had suspected me of being Jewish, they would surely betray me when I rejected their offer.

From afar, I spotted the police superintendent, my inquisitor. I froze. Germans rarely entered that park, and I was certain that he was there to take me to the police station. But he only glanced in my direction and galloped away. I relaxed and joined the others in a joyful conversation. Everyone had a story to tell about home, and I, the best pretender of all, was not short of one.

'I have about one hundred cousins,' I told them. 'Nearly all of them are boys. I can just imagine the fuss they are going to make over me when I get home.' This I made sure to say within earshot of Marysia and her husband.

'They will all propose to you,' they said. 'Because by then, you will have become a famous writer.'

I could see Marysia's face sadden. She wanted me in her family and realised that this probably would not be likely. Still, she treated me as if I were her relative already.

'You said you lost your rosary,' she said. 'So we bought you one.'

'How kind you are. This is something I really need.'

I made my way home to the Perlmutts, to Sonnen Strasse 9. I greeted everyone, showing off my new rosary. If they saw it, they would believe I went to church on Sundays. None of them knew that I did not go because I always told them I went with my Polish friends.

I left the rosary on top of my dressing table so that if the Perlmutts decided to look in my room in my absence they would notice it, and then tell all the others.

As I lay in my bed that night, I wondered if I should perhaps try to run away, but that did not seem such a good idea. I would soon be recaptured, perhaps even the same day. I was on German soil and nowhere near Polish villages. My situation was now more serious than it had been in Poland. Although I was living in a house among people, I felt very much as if I were still alone in a dark and dangerous forest. The people among whom I found myself were certainly not my friends. They were dangerous predators, far more dangerous than any of the animals I had encountered in the Polish forest.

During the following week, no one bothered me. I imagined the Ukrainians were watching every step I made, but I pretended not to notice. I wondered why I had not yet been arrested. What were the Germans waiting for? There was only one answer: they were making inquiries in Janów, and that took time. They would know where to find me when the information arrived. Meanwhile, I put on a different dress every day so as not to leave any clean ones to my enemies when the Nazis came to arrest me.

One German worker asked me why I dressed up all the time. She reminded me that I was not going to church every day but doing dirty work.

'I like dressing up,' I told her. 'And I have many dresses, as you can see.'

'Yes, we noticed this already,' she said. 'And we think you have become very funny suddenly, unless you're expecting Prince Charming to come through the door.'

I pretended to become very sad. 'The boys don't really like me,' I told her.

She suddenly seemed to feel sorry for me and probably thought I was dressing up because I suffered from an inferiority complex, which I certainly did not. I was relieved to see that my answer satisfied her curiosity.

The superintendent from the police station had begun frequenting the Perlmutts' guest house. Every time he came into the restaurant to eat or drink, he stopped in the kitchen to greet Frau Perlmutt. That was no more than a transparent ruse, for he always gave me a secret look. I failed to comprehend why he had not yet reported his suspicions. It occurred to me that he may have done so already and that the matter was now out of his hands. I was certain that in a day or two I would be taken away.

I became more and more fearful and tried to bolster my morale. I was a very big fighter, I remembered. And they only had a suspicion that I was Jewish. Had they been certain, they would already have arrested and tortured me. I was more afraid of torture than death.

Thoughts of my impending arrest occupied my mind that whole week. By the time Sunday arrived, I was filled with trepidation at the thought of going to the police station to sign in. There was no choice, however, but to go.

As I entered the building, I plucked up courage and forced myself to appear indifferent to my interrogator. I had put on a nice dress and appeared quite happy outwardly. How surprised I was to see that the superintendent had now prepared two cups of coffee and some cake and invited me to sit down and join him in a snack. He was as friendly as he had been the previous week, but to my great dismay, he suddenly announced: 'You know, Stefin, the Jews in Lublin sounded exactly like you.'

Gathering all my strength and putting on the most innocent expression I could muster, I replied, 'What are Jews, sir?' as if they did not genuinely concern me.

'You really mean to say that you don't know what Jews are?' he asked with false amazement.

He did not really expect an answer, and I did not offer one. Instead, I reminded him that German boys were not allowed to speak to Polish girls. Immediately, I regretted what I had said when I reminded myself that he did not really see me as a girl, but as a Jew. But if that were the case, why had he laid out those treats for me? I became more and more puzzled and decided that either he could not be sure that I was Jewish or he simply did not want me to die.

The following Saturday night, I hardly slept. I was trying to think of a way to convince the officer that I was not Jewish, and that was no easy matter.

Sunday, I once more entered the police station with a

big smile and head held high. This time, I did not wait for the officer to address me but spoke first, pretending that I was not in the least concerned.

'Last week, you wanted to know what Jews were, sir, and my Polish friends explained to me in detail what they really look like.' I smiled. 'My friends told me that they have dark eyes and dark hair, just like you have, sir.' I then pushed my luck a little further and cheekily asked him why he was so interested in Jews.

He returned my smile and said no more.

I did not really believe I had accomplished very much and still expected a visit from a higher authority. I believed that Marysia and her Ukrainian husband had attempted to betray me. Hadn't the superintendent said that the people who betrayed me were not my friends? I concluded that it could only have been Marysia and her husband. All their conversation about a cousin from Bitterfeld had been a trick. They were not genuine friends, but rather my enemies, I decided.

The following Sunday, I was determined to appear even more unconcerned, and on entering the police station, I went straight to the superintendent and said, 'I hope you're not going to ask me the same silly questions again today, sir. For a change, why don't you ask the others who are waiting outside? I have no time for you today. It's my day off, and my friends are waiting for me.'

Saying so, and not without some trepidation in my heart, I turned on my heels and flounced out of his office as fast as I could. I was expecting to be followed because I had been quite rude, but he did not come after me.

I soon regretted what I did, and I almost went back to him to apologise, but the Polish and Ukrainian girls in the outer room besieged me with questions before I could do so.

'Why do you stay in there so long?' they asked. 'Look at us. We just go in and out. Are you by any chance informing on us? We're not allowed to speak to him, and he's not allowed to speak to us,' they reminded me.

'I know,' I said. 'Next time I must tell him this.'

'Does he want to marry you by any chance?'

I laughed. 'I don't think he's in the least interested in me. I'm only a Polish worm.'

A girl named Helena bristled and asked, 'What did you say?'

'Oh, that's what a German boy once called me when he found out that I was Polish.'

Her face became suffused with rage, and she ground her teeth in anger. The others swore at Germans as loudly as they dared.

'A Polish worm, indeed! We are far better than they are, and one day, we shall have our own country back.'

'I'm sure we will,' I answered, which cheered them all up.

'He doesn't deserve such a nice girl like you, that's for sure. And you should marry a Polish boy. Like Tadeusz. He's a nice boy. We know that he proposed to you, but you refused him.'

'I have to go back to school before I can think of marriage,' I answered. 'I haven't even finished my elementary education.'

'And you still have to write that book,' someone reminded me.

'I have not forgotten that,' I said.

Then, wanting to keep her mind off the superintendent, I said, 'I wonder how long it will take before we are reunited with our poor families. I so long to go home. What about all of you . . . ?' I wanted to reassure them that I was not going to marry a German boy, our enemy.

The following Sunday, there was a new officer at the station who expressed no particular interest in me. I was relieved but wondered who would torment me next.

One day, I heard a radio broadcast about how the Warsaw Ghetto was burning and all the Jewish people were dying in their houses. Instinctively, I stopped work for a few moments, whereupon one of the hotel workers became suspicious and challenged me about understanding so much German. Thinking quickly, I replied that I had picked up a few words about a Warsaw theatre group. The German girl then laughed heartily, and with gleeful satisfaction, repeated the painful news that I had already understood myself. I could not show any emotion or any interest in those events, and I would have to pretend that my German was still lacking.

The next time Frau Perlmutt asked me to bring her an egg from the pantry, I asked her what that was. When she told me that it was round and white, I deliberately brought a round white loaf of bread.

'I told you, it is quite small,' Frau Perlmutt repeated once again.

This time I brought her a roll.

Frau Perlmutt became quite exasperated with me and she sent another worker to bring the egg, saying that I was so stupid that I would never master the German language.

'*Die ist doch zu blöd auch nur etwas zu kapieren,*' Herr Perlmutt remarked with a red face. 'She is too stupid to understand even the most elementary of words.' Frau Perlmutt, however, told him and my co-workers that all was not yet lost. She reminded them how clever I was to have made myself curtains with large sheets of tracing paper; even the neighbours came to admire them, and the rest of my tidy bedroom. One of the neighbours confided in Frau Perlmutt that she too could do with a girl like me and that she would take me if Frau Perlmutt no longer wanted me. But Frau Perlmutt was not willing to give me up yet and said, 'She works like a machine once switched on, though it's true she does not always remember her own name, and that surprises me.'

After Frau Perlmutt's compliment, I thought it would be safe to show a little more understanding of German and within a few months, Frau Perlmutt delighted in conducting reasonably long conversations with me.

'You know, Stefin,' she used to say, 'I always believed that you have more intelligence in you. It was only the language difficulty that convinced us that you were ignorant.'

I was determined to work even harder and save the Perlmutts as much money as I could. They would not need the window-washer, for I showed that I was not afraid of heights and was willing to risk my life and clean all the windows, inside and out.

There was only one job which I hated: displaying *Der Stürmer*, a vile anti-Semitic magazine, for all the soldiers to read. The magazines depicted Jews as having such ugly faces that they were almost unrecognisable as human beings. After seeing those magazines, I would sometimes go upstairs to my bedroom and look at myself in the mirror, satisfying myself that I did not resemble any of those horrible sketches. Nor had my beautiful sisters and friends resembled any of them.

Thinking of those caricatures in the magazines, I would become so angry that I could hardly sleep. I failed to understand how a nation which excelled in music and literature could be so stupid as to believe that the pictures were accurate portrayals of Jewish people. How could they sink lower than vermin in such a short space of time? How could they play to the tune of one person's music, a person to whom they abandoned all their own brains?

My parents had often taught us that 'a young mind is soft and is therefore easily bent. While we are growing, we sometimes copy good things from people, but often also bad ones. Always stay with good friends, and you will grow up good,' my parents used to say.

Only then did I fully understand what they meant.

23. Besting an Officer

After some time, my German became quite fluent, and I began to sound a bit like a native. In the Perlmutts' eyes, I had left my stupidity behind. They became very fond of me, and they allowed me out of the hotel more and more frequently. The hotel was closed on Thursday afternoons, and I was free to go out after I finished my chores. There was, of course, a curfew. Foreign workers were not permitted outdoors after eight o'clock in the evening. They also had to wear badges on their lapels. The Poles had the letter *P* sewn on to their left lapels and were not permitted to leave the house without displaying it. Foreign workers were prohibited from travelling outside their assigned towns, so I was expected to remain in the town I was assigned to all the time.

But I removed the *P* on many occasions, as I had done in Poland with my yellow Star of David, and ventured outside unnoticed. Sometimes, I went to the hairdressers, where I was thought of as a German girl. At other times, I went to a dressmaker, a kind young woman who, for some reason, gave me dresses for free. On rare occasions, when my courage was high, I also went to the cinema. It was strictly forbidden to us, but I risked going because it was the only place I could hear uninterrupted news of the war.

Some of my Polish acquaintances had been reassigned from the chocolate factory to a farm near us. There may have been a train which went there, but since it was forbidden for me to travel out of town, I never inquired about it. Not having anything particular to do one day, I plucked up the courage and decided to walk to that farm.

In the same village, not far from the farm, there was a Russian POW camp with pitifully emaciated prisoners who resembled starved animals more than human beings. I knew quite well what it was like to be hungry, and I was determined to help those poor Russians, whatever the risks.

The next free Sunday, I took some bread and butter and a whole side of bacon from the hotel pantry and set off. Upon my arrival, I went first to the POW camp and pushed the food through the railings.

'*Spasibo, spasibo, diewushka!*' they all called out. 'Thank you, thank you, young lady!' They had no knives to cut the bacon and attacked the food like hungry vultures.

I felt a great satisfaction in feeding them. I knew quite well what risk I was taking, but that was my specialty. No one was better at it than I was, and if stealing to feed such starving people was a sin, then I was prepared to be punished for it.

I took a quick look around before I left and thought I was safe. But as I walked to my friends at the farm, I saw a German lady looking at me in a suspicious manner. She seemed to know that I was a stranger and that I should have been wearing a *P* on my lapel.

A few hours later, a police officer arrived and immediately set to searching my bag. He found nothing in it but my handkerchief. He took me in his horse-drawn cart back to town. He did not utter a word along the way; occasionally, he turned round and gave me a hostile look. I returned his looks and was not really afraid. I knew that whatever my punishment would be, it would not be the death sentence, for he had no idea I had given food to the Russians.

He dropped me near his police station and threatened that I would hear from him in due course. But I did not believe that I would ever see or hear of him again, which was a little naive of me.

He came to the hotel a few days later. At the time, I was in the wash-house, helping with the laundry. He presented me with a charge sheet in which I was accused of removing my *P* badge and travelling out of town.

I knew that I was a useful slave and that my life was not so much in danger. I summoned my stoniest expression and said to the officer, 'This charge sheet will one day be framed and hung in my living room for everyone to see what crimes I committed. Of course, I removed the *P*. I could not have left town with it to visit my beloved friends – a very big crime indeed!'

He tried to take the sheet of paper away from me, which got torn to pieces in the process. He seemed at a loss, and I thought he looked a little afraid, probably realising that I already knew too much.

Having mixed with many Germans who assumed I was one of them, I had learned that their army was no

194

longer winning on all fronts. I understood quite well that they were already on the losing side. Their mighty Führer seemed to be shrinking, and it was only a matter of time before he would be defeated. I sincerely hoped that I would manage to live to see the liberation of the persecuted and the fall of those mighty executioners and their beloved Führer.

I was very eager to find out more about the current situation but had few means to do so. I was not supposed to listen to the news, as if it did not really concern me; and the Germans had become afraid to discuss the situation even among themselves. It was strictly forbidden to lose faith in Hitler, a crime for which they were put on the 'blacklist', eventually to be punished by shooting or other serious penalties. It was also strictly forbidden for Germans to listen to foreign stations on the wireless, but many did, at great risk to themselves.

The officer who had come with his charge sheet could now see for himself what all foreigners already realised. He was probably worried about what might happen to him after the war ended. He looked more afraid than infuriated, and that suited me quite well as I became even more hopeful for survival.

He let the matter drop, and everyone could see that I had frightened a heavily decorated officer.

24. Glimmers of Hope

The huge cellar in the hotel was divided into various sections. One of them served as a shelter where everyone waited out air raids; the second was a storehouse for barrels of beer; and the third contained freshly baked bread and cakes. There were also cupboards for storing some of our clothing, in case everything above the cellar was destroyed by bombs.

The smell of the bread became too much of a temptation for me one day, and I devised a way of satisfying my appetite. We were fed three times a day, but I was a hard worker and needed more. Besides, the other workers managed to get some help from their parents.

Early one Sunday morning, when everyone was still asleep, I tiptoed barefoot down to the cellar and took one of my dresses from the cellar cupboard. I then cut a big chunk of cake and also took a large loaf of bread and wrapped them both in my dress. I switched off the light and ran upstairs with my provisions.

I met with the stable man, an elderly man who worked very hard for his age. He was rubbing his eyes and seemed very tired. In addition to feeding the horses, he also had to groom them. He was from old stock and was by nature quite a kind man. Hitler had not changed him.

'*Guten Morgen, Herr Storzman*,' I said to the bewildered gentleman in a most friendly, innocent tone.

'What are you doing here so early in the morning?' he wanted to know.

'I did not sleep very well after the air raid,' I told him. 'I spent the night thinking about which dress I would wear today. Today is Sunday, you know.'

Herr Storzman did not express any doubts as to the sincerity of my story, and I continued upstairs. However, I remembered that in the confusion I had left another loaf of bread in a place it should not have been. Although my punishment would not have been severe, I did not want to be known as a thief because I would then be watched more closely and my good name would be blemished. Fearful of being discovered as a thief, I took another risk and went down once more with the dress. Herr Storzman still stood there, and I told him I had taken the wrong dress and needed to go down to change it.

I was now quite careful to hide the second loaf of bread under the new dress, a nice woollen one, which I then had to wear. Unfortunately, it was summer, and I looked most ridiculous for the first hours of the day; it wasn't until the afternoon that I managed to change my woollen dress for a more summery one. But no one noticed the woollen dress, or the summery one. They had other things to consider.

Air raids were now increasing in intensity, and hardly a night passed without British planes coming to bomb the nearby larger towns. The American bombers came during the day. Since we were permitted only German radio stations, news of the Allies' advance travelled very slowly our way. But on many occasions, I caught sight of Herr Perlmutt secretly listening to foreign stations.

He had also started answering soldiers' greetings with '*Guten Morgen,*' instead of the usual '*Heil Hitler.*'

The young, brain-washed boys whom he fed did not take kindly to this display of 'treason' and threatened him openly. 'Wait until the war is over,' they would say. 'You are on the blacklist.' This implied that he would be severely punished for his crimes, probably by death, and I wondered whether the Germans would kill their own people, as well.

I began to understand what a ruthless leader Hitler really was. Taking a life from a person meant nothing to him – not even if it was a German life – and all those young soldiers followed him obediently, their humanity long forgotten.

On several occasions, I overheard soldiers joking about their Japanese allies. 'They really believe we are going to share everything with them,' one soldier said.

'Let them,' said another. 'We need them now. We know what to do with them later on,' and they laughed heartily.

But cracks appeared in their bravado; they sometimes sang a song that showed they did not really believe they would win the war:

> *Schön ist die Nacht,*
> *Der Himmel bewacht;*
> *Die Englische Flüge kommen schon wieder zu uns,*

nur jeder Nacht.
Beautiful is the night,
The heavens so bright,
The English planes are coming again,
They come every night.

While they were lamenting, I was secretly rejoicing and becoming more and more hopeful for survival. I also longed for more news, which I could not get from my co-workers.

On one of my free days, I picked up Malach and decided on an impulse to travel to Leipzig, which I had visited a few times. I was, of course, quite nervous and hoped I would not meet people who knew I was Polish.

The train was crowded, so I had no choice but to sit with other people, Germans of course. On the outward journey, I sat between two soldiers. They naturally thought that I was a German girl and struck up a conversation with me. I was worried that they might detect that German was not my mother tongue, so I quickly asked them which part of Germany they came from. After they answered, I told them that I came from a completely different part of the country, thus explaining my accent.

'Listen to her, she does speak with a different accent,' one said.

'I don't care about her accent,' said the other one. 'She speaks beautifully, and I like it.'

And after that, I pretended that I had been offended

by their familiarity and moved to a seat where there were only older people on either side of me.

On arrival at Leipzig, I went straight to the zoo, enjoying the sunshine and the innocence of the animals. I began feeding the monkeys, and three girls stopped to chat with me.

They shared a room in cheap accommodation, they said, and I asked if they would mind if I joined them for one night. I had quarrelled with my stepmother that morning, I told them, and I did not want to return to her tonight.

They were all quite happy for some new company and agreed to my request. I was overjoyed. I was eager to find out how the war was progressing, and here was a very good opportunity. I wanted to get more information about the Allies' advance and did not care about the consequences of my actions and what might happen to me when I returned to the hotel. I made up my mind to play a seemingly unintelligent girl who was not really interested in politics and whose only worry was my bad stepmother.

One of the girls looked sad and wore a black armband. She told me that her fiancé had recently been killed near Kraków and that the Germans were now retreating. I rejoiced silently and wished one member of my family had also managed to survive. Only now did I begin to realise how lonely I would feel in the future. I began to question my wisdom at having struggled so ferociously to survive. I shook myself as if from a dream when I realised I was losing hope. To lose hope now, I decided, was foolish. Now I was going to have my freedom at long last, and I would tell the world what human beings were capable of doing.

After chatting awhile in their hotel room, I decided to lie down and pretend I was sleeping. I knew that they would soon start conversing with each other freely, and I would be able to hear for the first time how the situation really was. I deliberately began snoring to convince them that I was truly fast asleep.

As expected, they soon started conversing with each other. The girl who had lost her fiancé began to complain bitterly that Hitler was deceiving them. They seemed to have lost all hope of German victory. I could not believe my good fortune and strained my ears to listen to everything they had to say, making sure I did not even stir.

Soon, they all began to cry. How glad I was to see that it was also their turn to be unhappy. I somehow felt that I had to exert my authority over the girls and make them a little frightened of German soldiers like I had been for all those years. I picked up my head from under the blankets and began to chastise them sternly.

'Did I hear you complaining about Hitler?' I asked. 'Have you lost all faith in our Führer? Why, you don't sound like German girls at all. You ought to be ashamed of yourselves!'

They were utterly puzzled by my sudden and violent expression of emotion. They all looked at me apprehensively, fearful that I was some sort of spy and would report them to my superior. They gave me presents and begged me not to tell anyone what I had just overheard. I soon apologised and asked them kindly for some food, after which I fell into a deep slumber with a light heart. When I awoke, I thanked them all kindly and assured them that I would not report them.

I soon went to the station, practically dancing all the way. People stared at me, but I did not really care if they thought me feeble or even crazy.

The intoxicating thought of freedom that cheered me on my way home was soon dispelled by thoughts of the uncertain future I would have to face once the war was over. I had seen my home, my family and my people savagely destroyed by barbaric hordes, and I had become a slave and fugitive among strange people. What would I do after the war? Where would I go? I wondered.

On my return to the hotel, I was admonished by my employers for not having returned the previous night, but I did not respond and let them believe whatever they wanted. The most important thing was that I still had my job and that they were very pleased to see me back. For the time being, this was still my home, and I was pleased to enter my room. I changed my dress and went downstairs to work. I found I could now smile at all of them, not caring whether they smiled back at me or not. No one even bothered to ask me why my mood had suddenly changed. In view of the worsening situation, I was no longer the centre of attention.

The hotel staff were all greatly upset with the way the war was going for them, and they began to speak to me with greater respect all the time. The way they treated me did not matter to me any more; I now dreamed of freedom and was determined not to remain in Germany a minute longer than was necessary. My dreams took me to Palestine, where I would be starting a new life with my own people.

One Thursday afternoon, while I was enjoying a leisurely stroll through the town, a middle-aged German couple engaged me in conversation. They introduced themselves as Herr and Frau Ehrhardt. The name intrigued me because I had heard of a Jewish family with that name. How disappointed I was to learn about their Protestant origins. They invited me to their house for tea on the following Sunday afternoon, telling me that they had no children and that they liked intelligent conversation. Somehow, I felt attracted to them, and I needed company even more than they did. This couple appeared to be genuinely lonely, but I wondered why they chose me, a complete stranger.

When I entered their house, I saw that it was very tidy and knew they did not want me to keep house for them. They seemed genuine enough in their desire for friendship, yet I began to question my wisdom in accepting an invitation from complete strangers. When I left, they asked me to come again on any free day, and they bid me a very friendly farewell.

The next Sunday, I put on a nice dress and went to see the Ehrhardts once more. I enjoyed the relaxed atmosphere in their beautiful garden very much, and our conversations touched on every subject under the sun except the war and politics. Noticing my interest as I stared at the crowded bookshelves in their study, Herr Ehrhardt offered to lend me some books. He showed me some German classics and some volumes of Shakespeare, which my sister Balla used to read. She had kept those books for me so that I could read them when I grew older. I had not even read one page. And now here were all those books. Yet I hesitated to take them, not being sure if I should reveal that I could read some German.

Again, I wondered if the Ehrhardts were genuinely friendly or had been put up by the police to spy on me. I knew they could not do much harm to me now; Pikule, my adopted birthplace, had long been occupied by the Russian Army, and it was impossible for the Germans to obtain information about my true identity now. But what if the situation reversed itself and the Germans reoccupied that area again? There was nothing for me to do but pray and hope for the best.

Being lonely, I continued going to the Ehrhardts on many occasions, and I became very fond of them. Frau Ehrhardt reminded me of my Auntie Suri, my grandfather's sister, who also had no children and always made a big fuss over me. The Ehrhardts treated me as if I were a special girl, preparing my favourite foods and buying me pretty dresses now and then. Even so, I could not shake the thought that they might have been spying on me, either for the Perlmutts or the police.

I made up my mind to observe them more closely on my next visit just as they may have observed me. As far as I could see, they were kind people who appeared to feel sorry for such a young girl who was uprooted from her family. But I could not understand why they had chosen me. It was not too long, however, before I found out.

One Sunday, they gave me a nice necklace. Frau Ehrhardt waited a few minutes while I admired the trinket and said, 'You may wonder, Stefin, how we came to hear about you.'

I did not want them to know how much I was speculating why they had befriended me in particular, there being so many prettier Polish girls in town.

'What we are going to disclose to you now, Stefin dear, must remain a secret,' she went on. 'The superintendent at the police station who used to detain you is a friend of our family. He is waiting for the war to end; then he will be able to propose to you. You probably know that right now the situation is such that a German boy is not even allowed to speak to a foreign girl.'

'I know,' I told them. 'I also reminded that officer at the station about it. I did not want to get myself in trouble either. But I am only a Polish worker. I am a strictly practising Catholic, and all members of the Wehrmacht are non-believers.'

'Stefin dear,' she said, 'we are so sorry to admit to you, but we know that you have only attended church once with the Perlmutts. On Christmas Eve, 1942.'

So they really had been spying on me! How foolish I was to believe that I would survive. I began to wonder where I had gone wrong. I must have done something to arouse their suspicions, but I could not recollect what that might have been. Whatever it was, I would have to try to find out how the Ehrhardts had discovered that I did not go to church.

After mulling it over for a long time, I came to the conclusion that one of my Polish friends had somehow betrayed me. I began to scrutinise every girl I knew and decided to discount them all. If even one person had had a suspicion that I was Jewish, it would have become general knowledge. In that case, I would not have lasted until now.

Suddenly, I remembered that once when a neighbour of the Perlmutts had complimented me on my good German pronunciation, I had jokingly said that I came from 'Deitschland', the Yiddish pronunciation of 'Deutschland'. She probably told this to the Perlmutts who, in turn, informed the police about it.

It was no good keeping away from the Ehrhardts now, and I decided to pay them another visit.

'Isn't the weather wonderful?' remarked Herr Ehrhardt as he invited me to sit down.

We were sitting in their beautiful garden, and the table was festively decorated, as if for a special occasion. Hesitatingly, I inquired if we were perhaps having a birthday party, whereupon Herr Ehrhardt replied that it could become some sort of celebration if I would only agree.

'Agree to what?' I asked.

'We have no children of our own,' Herr Ehrhardt said suddenly. 'We would love to adopt you, Stefin dear.'

I was now really flabbergasted, for despite my fondness of them and the warmth they had shown me, I had not expected this situation and became very frightened to refuse. But I knew that I must because I had not forgotten who I was and wanted to remain Jewish. Had I wanted to convert, I had only to go to the priests, who would have managed to hide me in a church as a nun. But I was from a strictly Orthodox family and would have rather died than allow myself to be converted.

This situation was quite difficult for me, and a lot of hard thinking lay ahead. Once more, I was face to face with a difficult predicament.

I knew quite well what the consequences would be should they decide to pry deeper into my past. But the most important thing was that I did not want to be adopted by them. I thanked the Ehrhardts for their kindness and told them that I wanted to go back to my family after the war. I had come to like them very much, I said, but regretfully, my answer must be 'no'.

They said that they did understand, but should I ever change my mind, their offer would still stand. I continued to visit them as often as I could and called them Uncle and Aunt, which they seemed to love. It bothered me, though, how they knew I had no family. No one knew that except the superintendent.

One day, I saw some high-ranking German officers and several ordinary soldiers entering the hotel. They had left the front door open and, through the entrance, I could see about a hundred Russian prisoners outside in the square. They looked more dead than alive, and some of them were sitting in wheelbarrows which were pushed by their stronger friends. The Germans were not worried about leaving their charges unattended as the Russians hardly had the strength to stand up, let alone run away.

My heart went out to them, and I decided to help them a little.

Those Russians looked as if they hadn't eaten for a very long time, and while their guards ate and made themselves merry in the restaurant, I secretly entered the pantry, took some bread rolls and went out to the square. After breaking the rolls into small pieces, I threw them to the Russians. There was soon a great rush as the ones who could move pounced on the food. They only used their mouths as their hands appeared to be broken. I watched in horror; they looked just like chickens pecking at their feed with their beaks.

So that is what the human race can be reduced to, I thought. I wondered how many Jewish people had suffered the same fate. I felt like crying but did not want anyone to ask me why.

The Germans had consumed a fair amount of wine and whisky and were singing to their hearts' content; they did not even hear the commotion in the square. But Herr Perlmutt saw what I was doing. I am certain that he never told anyone about it, except possibly his wife. Neither of them asked me why I had decided to take such a risk, for they too must have been pleased I did it.

25. Shared Secrets

Early in 1945, an Italian family called Paci came to stay at the hotel. Their daughter Geena seemed forlorn, and I worked up the courage to talk to her.

'I'm Stefania,' I told her. 'I'm from Poland.'

'I'm Geena,' she introduced herself. 'And we're from Italy.'

'Your country resembles a boot on the map,' I said.

Geena laughed. 'You must have been very good at geography at school to remember this,' she said. 'Did you also study German in Poland? You speak it very well.'

'No,' I said. 'I couldn't speak a word of it when I first came here. It took a long time to learn it.'

'You speak German almost fluently. That's surprising for a Polish girl.'

'I've been here two and a half years, and I work with German girls.' I told her. 'But even though I speak their language, they don't want to become my friends.'

'They don't seem to like me very much, either,' Geena said.

That surprised me greatly because her father was a heavily decorated officer, and German girls loved soldiers, especially important ones.

Before very long, Geena and I became best friends. I

could see that she was not very happy. I suspected that there must have been a very good reason for that and tried to gain Geena's confidence.

'Why do you always look so miserable?' I asked her. 'I can see that something is bothering you.'

'I don't get on very well with my father,' she told me and declined to say any more.

Geena's parents often argued loudly, but since not one of us understood Italian, the reason for their quarrelling remained a secret. It seemed obvious to me, however, that it was Geena and her mother against the father.

As the days went by, I began to suspect that the Pacis were not ordinary people. They seemed rich, something I could tell from Geena's and her mother's hands, unlike mine, which looked twenty years older than the rest of my body. Their hands were well preserved, indicating that they were not used to doing much housework. Why, I wondered, should a seemingly well-off family such as the Pacis leave all their possessions behind and stay in one small room?

Eventually, Geena told me that they had had to run away from Italy. She did not offer to tell me the reason, but I decided that the political situation had caused them to flee. Although I felt sorry for Geena, I also knew that the more serious the situation became for them, the nearer freedom was for me.

The Pacis conversed freely with the Germans. As soon as I came around, however, they started talking about the weather. I began to suspect that they were talking about me. Had Mr Paci been sent to the hotel to spy on me? But if that were the case, then why had he brought his wife and daughter along with him? Perhaps Geena had been assigned to extract information from me, I suddenly suspected.

The worried expressions on their faces as they listened to the news on the radio made me realise that there must have been a different reason for their presence at the hotel. I could also see that the news did not please them. I soon decided that they were unhappy because things were beginning to look bad for them, and realised this was a good chance for me to find out more.

I invited Geena for a walk, hoping she would give me information to confirm my assessment of the situation. We set out for a stroll through the streets of the town, and I gave her an extra big smile. I knew she would not keep her grief to herself any longer.

'You look so sad, Geena, I wish there was something I could do to make you feel happier,' I said. 'Did anything terrible happen to your family? Have you lost anyone perhaps?'

'We lost plenty of relatives,' she replied. 'They were all in the army.'

'You mean they've been fighting the Germans for five years?' I asked innocently and deliberately.

Geena was still a bit suspicious and didn't answer me initially. Trying to sound sympathetic, I pushed my luck further.

'Were your relatives in the Nazi Party? Did they die fighting the Allies?'

Geena buried her head in her hands. 'You guessed right, Stefin, dear.'

'You're lucky,' I replied, 'Anyone who joins the Nazi party from an occupied country is very well looked after in Germany. Don't you like it here?'

'I hate it here. So does my mother. She didn't want my father to join the Nazi Party in the first place, but he wouldn't listen to her. We are both afraid of my father. He is a beast, and he has blood on his hands. He killed many people and ordered many deaths. Some of the people I went to school with and loved died because of him. He even killed my best friend. Would you believe it?'

I would, I thought, knowing better than anyone else what those *Herrenvolk* were capable of doing, and her father belonged to them.

After a few minutes, she said, 'I had quite forgotten that you're not German. My father told me as soon as we arrived at the hotel that I should be careful about what I say in your presence. But I like you better than him, and I'm ashamed to admit that he's my father.'

Realising what she had said, Geena suddenly paled. 'You must promise me that you won't say a word of what I have told you to anyone. I would be in a lot of trouble if someone discovered that I had discussed these things with a Polish girl. You won't say anything, will you? Promise me, Stefin.'

'I promise not talk to anyone about this. But tell me, is your father running away? Is anyone after him?'

Now that she had already entrusted me with so much information, there was no point in holding back. Tears began streaming down Geena's cheeks, and I lent her my clean handkerchief. I eagerly awaited what she was going to say next.

She again hesitated for a while as if words began to fail her, and sobbing quietly, she said, 'My father is running away from the advancing armies. He thinks the German Reich will soon be defeated.'

Her words were like music to me.

'Does it look like that's going to happen?' I asked. 'Do you really think Germany is going to lose this war?'

'Either the Americans or the Russians will be here soon,' she said. 'It may take a month or so, but they will be here. I am worried, Stefania, afraid of the revenge they will take on us. You come from a small town, and you don't know what it's like to be a fugitive, to have to hide and live in fear the whole time. I envy you, Stefin, dear.'

'But how can you be so sure that the Germans are going to lose the war?' I asked her, ignoring the irony of her comment. 'The situation could still be reversed. Then you'll be able to go back home.'

'I don't want the Germans to win. If they win, they'll kill half the Italian population. Whoever didn't collaborate with the Nazis is on the blacklist and will be killed. My mother and my cousins will all die. Whenever they argued with my father, he would say, "Just wait until the war's over; your day of reckoning will come yet." Now do you understand why I don't want the Germans to win the war?'

'I understand,' I told her and promised again not to tell anyone about our conversation, not even my Polish friends. 'You're now my closest friend, Geena. I liked you the minute I set eyes on you. Since I left my family, no one has been as close to me as you are.'

I looked guiltily at Malach, sitting quietly nearby.

We walked in the direction of the park, holding hands like sisters.

'*Noi andiamo*,' said Geena. 'That's Italian for "we are walking".'

'*My chodzimy*,' I told her the equivalent in Polish and reciprocated with a few more words in my mother tongue.

Geena was holding a newspaper. I caught sight of the date – March 19, 1945 – and for some reason, I became filled with an overwhelming need to tell someone my story, to share the burden of my sadness which I had carried in my torn heart for so many years. I debated inwardly for a while. I needed to share my secret, but the risk was so great. Finally, the urge to tell someone the truth overcame the need to be careful. I understood what risk I was now about to take and hoped that my judgement of Geena's character was correct. I prayed that she really was a good person to whom I could entrust my secret. I felt a shiver inside my lonely heart, knowing that I would either win a good friend or lose my life, even at this late hour when liberation was not so far away.

Geena must have seen the struggle on my face, for she asked, 'What is it, Stefin dear? Why have you suddenly gone quiet? Did I upset you with my tale? Please forgive me if I did.'

Hearing her gentle and reassuring words, I stood straight and looked directly into her eyes. 'Geena,' I said. 'Can you promise me that you will never tell anyone what I am going to disclose to you now?'

Geena nodded. Looking straight into her eyes, I felt reassured.

'I love you so much, Geena dear, as if you were my own sister. Once I had many sisters and a brother.'

Tears were streaming down my face now, wetting my dress and Geena's hands as she tried to dry my cheeks for me. I could see that she really did love me as only a sister could.

'My name is not Stefania, but Mala Szorer. I am Jewish, and I am all alone in the world now.'

Geena looked at me with disbelief.

'My entire family was killed by murderers like your father,' I continued. 'They killed my whole town's Jewish population – all my neighbours and friends.'

Geena looked at me with great compassion in her eyes. I felt certain that my secret would remain confidential. We cried together for a while and both experienced a common bond that nothing and no one could ever break. I felt an immense sense of relief, as if a giant boulder had suddenly been removed from my back. Even my fear that Geena would tell someone of my true identity vanished.

The sun was beginning to set when we decided to go home. We did not talk. We walked along, holding hands even more tightly than before. At last, we reached the place that had been my home for almost three years, my home amid the enemy, friendless, until Geena came along.

Dear Geena. Today I wonder if she will ever read my story and remember her friend Stefania who kept her word and did not disclose her secret to anyone for half a century. She, too, was faithful and did not tell anyone that I was Jewish. She was, after all, my best friend, like my faithful companion Malach.

26. A Jewish Soldier

The fighting came to German soil, and bombs were exploding every night in nearby towns. The sound was music to my ears because it meant that my redemption was not far off. I wanted to make plans for the future but could not imagine where to begin. It would take a long time to find myself again, yet I looked forward with great determination as only a young person can.

One night, heavy machine gun fire sounded right outside the hotel. I could not control my joy, and one of the workers shouted, 'Go to your room, you silly fool!' I was not such a fool as she imagined, but I said nothing to her. I had waited such a long time and now had the patience to wait just a little longer. I really wanted to be in my room now and was more than happy to comply, for there I could be alone and smile; I could even laugh out loud without anyone hearing me.

After a while, Geena joined me. She was worried about what might happen to her and her parents now.

'Nothing will happen to you, Geena,' I said. 'You're innocent, like those poor people who were killed. And I promised I would not denounce your father.'

I had intended to keep her story to myself as I had promised but made up my mind to give her father hostile looks when I next saw him. There was, however, little opportunity for that. The Allied troops approached the town, and the Pacis decided, quite hurriedly, to move on.

As Geena walked out of the door of the hotel, I felt a great emptiness inside me. She and her parents left in such a hurry that we didn't have time to part properly like the close friends we had become. But I will never forget her and still hope that we may one day meet and renew our friendship, a friendship which was born of mutual suffering. It was a friendship that had renewed my faith in human beings and taught me an important lesson: to judge people on their own merit or demerit, not on the merit or demerit of their ancestry.

After a fierce battle on April 20, 1945, our town was occupied by the Russians. I heard the people talk of the courage of the German soldiers as they struggled to withstand the Russian onslaught. I heard some of them say that they fought to the last drop of blood as Hitler had instructed them to do. Others supposedly shouted, '*Heil Hitler*,' and then shot themselves rather than face humiliation. I was not in the least interested in tales of courage and of how individuals had dealt with being vanquished. I focused on the absence of the slogan '*Deutschland siegt auf allen Fronten* – Germany is winning on all fronts.' I never heard it again.

It did not take long before all the foreign labourers began looting the German shops and businesses. When they came to our hotel, they asked me to help them steal all the Perlmutts' whisky and go celebrate with them in the streets. I begged them to go away, telling them that the Perlmutts were decent people who had given a Russian prisoner an old coat and a cap to keep him warm. This seemed to placate them, and they forgot about the whisky.

The Russian liberators allowed the refugees to take anything they wanted, in particular food and drinks from the Germans. Every day, Frau Perlmutt had new stories to tell of girls leaving for Poland with their hosts' jewellery, dresses and valuable household goods. The Perlmutts thanked me for my years of service and wanted to give me a few things from their possessions. They were amazed when I declined. I did not yet tell them that I was Jewish and continued working as before. They wondered why I was not contemplating going home like the others, but I found it impossible to talk about it yet, bursting into tears every time the subject came up. Although our town was already in the hands of the Russians, the war had not yet ended. I did not yet feel free; I was still fearful that the Germans would reoccupy our town, and I would be in the frying pan once more.

After a week of Russian occupation, the Americans took over. They posted sentries outside our hotel, changing guards every few hours. One evening, one of their soldiers came into the hotel. Speaking in German, he told everyone how German soldiers had shot the wounded Allied soldiers as well as some of the civilian prisoners they had taken. Frau Perlmutt lowered her face as if ashamed of what her own nation was capable of doing. Her own son was a soldier.

Unlike German soldiers after their triumph, the Americans had no wish to humiliate innocent civilians. An American soldier offered the Perlmutts and the hotel staff American cigarettes and paid for a round of drinks in dollars, a gesture so unexpected that the Perlmutts stared in disbelief at the green banknotes. Such an act of generosity was too much to comprehend, especially since Berlin was still in German hands.

The soldier introduced himself as David, and I almost gasped out loud. Then, he told them about his home in New York and took out some photographs he had in one of his pockets. He showed them a few pictures of his *Mutter*, his *Vater*, his *Schwestern* and, stammering a little, he pointed at a picture of his *Kalle*.

'What is a *Kalle*?' they asked.

'*Braut*, bride,' I blurted out. *Kalle* was not a German word.

They all stared at me, greatly surprised that I understood what they believed was spoken in English. One girl in particular did not take her eyes off me. I could read the question in her eyes: 'How did an uneducated Polish girl understand English?' She began whispering to the others, but I did not really care. Still, I decided to keep quiet.

David also looked at me in amazement, probably wondering how I alone had understood. I soon asked him to join me outside in the corridor, and when we were safely out of earshot of the others, I poured my heart out to him. I could not hold back now, for here was the first Jewish person I had seen in a long time. I soon began to cry uncontrollably, and I saw tears in his eyes, too. While I was still afraid to admit to the others that I was Jewish, he seemed not at all concerned or worried. I briefly told him how much I had suffered, and what the Germans had done to our people.

'One day,' I told him, 'I want the whole world to know about it.'

Until that time, I had believed I was the only Jewish person in Nazi-occupied Europe who had survived the Holocaust. How happy I was to learn from this soldier that there were still many Jewish people in the world; that *Hashem* would never allow all the Jewish people to perish.

'You probably don't realise that the war is not yet over,' he said. 'Berlin has not yet been taken; and we still have a long battle ahead of us with the Japanese who carry out suicidal missions. They're even worse than the Germans. They don't want to surrender and aren't even afraid to die.'

'It is a pity they don't know what I know,' I said.

I told him I had overheard some German soldiers mocking the Japanese, boasting about using them for the time being and predicting their eventual defeat.

'Maybe if the Japanese knew about that,' he said, 'the war would end immediately. Right now, we still have a big fight in front of us.'

I was still at a complete loss as to what I would do when the war would end and Germany was at last defeated. Where would I turn? I knew I would then need help from older and more experienced people. I would need money and a true identity card.

'Can you advise me about what to do when the war ends?' I asked the Jewish soldier. 'I don't want to stay here forever.'

'I will personally see to it that you don't have to remain in Germany one day longer than is necessary,' he replied.

He promised to write to his parents right away to ask them to invite me to come to America.

I could not believe my good fortune and went to share it with my cat who was waiting for me outside. 'If I go to America,' I told Malach, 'I shall take you with me, even if everyone will stare and think me insane. I will tell all of them how you kept me company and with *Hashem*'s help protected me for so many years.'

27. My Name Is Mala Szorer

The next day I went to see my dressmaker and asked her to make up some dresses for me. She had become a good friend who had sewn several beautiful dresses for me without pay. The dresses had made me the envy of all my Polish friends. They always asked to be introduced to the dressmaker; however, when I had asked if she would make up some dresses for the other girls, she always kept quiet. At the time, I did not know that those dresses were later to help keep me alive in Poland after the war.

I looked at myself in the mirror and saw that I was no longer a child. I was now seventeen-and-a-half years old and quite grown up in my mind, unlike children who grew up with their parents. I longed for such a life once more, but I knew I would continue having to fend for myself.

The following day, David brought me some tasty biscuits and cans of food. The cans had 'kosher' written on them, and I stared happily at the words. They were the first Hebrew letters I had seen since leaving Tarnogród.

The others became quite jealous and thought that David had become taken with me. I kept quiet and daydreamed about being at David's wedding and wishing him and his *kalle* a *mazel tov*.

Perhaps in America I, too, would meet a Jewish boy who would want to marry me. I became quite excited thinking about it. Perhaps I could still have a home and family of my own. Closing my eyes, I began to imagine what it would feel like. I began to see life, and not death, in front of me and longed to be reunited with my own people.

The next Friday, David came to the hotel with *challos* and wine. The Perlmutts overheard him reciting *Kiddush*, and they began asking me questions, not understanding what it was all about.

The war was not over yet, and I was still quite afraid to reveal my real identity to them. All those years of living a double life had left their mark on me. I was still fearful that they might do me some harm if they discovered that I was Jewish.

However, before I had time to respond to the Perlmutts' questions, David announced in German, 'Stefania is not what you think she is. She is a Jewish girl whose entire family was murdered by your soldiers. Her name is Mala.'

But if David thought that I was going to get any sympathy from the German workers in the hotel, he was very much mistaken.

'Tell me another lie,' one of them taunted.

'I shall never believe anything she says any more,' said another.

'What a liar she is!' added a third. 'Who would have believed it?'

Frau Perlmutt came up to me and held my hands, for

she alone understood what I had been through. I cried on her shoulder, then ran upstairs to my room and continued crying until my eyes dried up. Exhausted, I fell asleep and dreamed of home, of my dear parents and all the others.

When I awoke the following morning, I realised that I could not stay in my room indefinitely. Until my ticket to America arrived, I would still need to stay in the hotel and earn my keep. The Perlmutts were not obliged to let me stay, but I could not imagine that they would turn me out into the street, not now when they were losing the war.

Without hesitation, I went downstairs to ask for permission to stay a while longer, wondering how the others would react. I had seen their reaction when David revealed my true identity, and I did not expect too much sympathy from them now. I fully expected to be the centre of much hostile attention. In whatever manner they would treat me, I would be as friendly as I had always been but would keep my head held high. Now that they knew I was Jewish, I would have to show them that I belonged to a people who were compassionate; I would show them that I would not try to take revenge for their people's behaviour.

Herr and Frau Perlmutt were already waiting for me and, with a reassuring smile, invited me to have breakfast with them. They listened intently as I unfolded the story of the tragedies that had befallen my people.

After the meal, I returned to my room, intending to catch-up on some sleep. It was *Shabbos*, and I would not work. Frau Perlmutt followed me upstairs. She sat down on my bed and said that I would not have to do any work and could stay at the hotel until I decided what I wanted to do next. I told her David's parents would send me a ticket to America, and I expected to hear from them very soon.

As far as I was concerned, I was almost in America, even if my ticket had not yet arrived. I had no idea how long it took for a letter to arrive from America, but I would wait happily and daydream about what my new country would be like. I hoped David's parents would turn out to be as nice as he was, but at the same time, I had full confidence that I could fend for myself.

How disappointed I was the next morning. Instead of David, a tall American soldier by the name of Wacek came to the hotel. He spoke Czech, which is a bit similar to Polish, so we were able to converse. He said that David had been posted to Japan and had asked him to bring a parcel to me and to look after me. The parcel was packed with kosher food. I knew that since David must have had to leave very quickly, he probably had not had the time to contact his parents.

Not allowing my disappointment to get the better of me, I asked Wacek where I might be able to find some Jewish people.

'Try Halle,' he said. 'It is a much bigger town. I'll try to get a permit for you from my headquarters.'

The next day, Wacek handed me a travel permit and said, 'See if you can meet some concentration camp survivors and join them. I cannot take you there myself because I've been stationed here. I wish you lots of luck.'

As grateful as I was for his help, I was glad that Wacek could not accompany me. I was accustomed to looking after myself and had no fear of travelling alone.

I was excited that I could meet some Jewish people in Halle. Could it really be true, I wondered, that other Jewish people have survived? The time for Hitler to salute the only Jew left alive in 1944 had long passed. I knew that the war was not over, but I heard that it soon would be.

I packed all my belongings and said goodbye to the Perlmutts, truly believing I would never return. Soon, I was running to the station. I was running effortlessly; I was flying. I could not get away fast enough.

The train was filled with sad faces. People were staring at each other and looking forlorn.

I took a seat next to an older woman, who immediately asked, '*Ist das nicht furchtbar*? Isn't this terrible?'

I decided not to answer her and soon fell fast asleep. I dreamed of my freedom and must have talked in my sleep, for the woman suddenly asked, 'What did you say your name was?'

'What do you mean?' I asked defensively.

'You said your name was not Stefania something,' she replied.

Straightening my back and holding my head high, I said out loud, clearly emphasising every syllable, 'It isn't. My name is not Stefania Iwkiewicz. It is Mala Szorer.'

'What a funny name you have. It's not a German name.'

'No, it is not a German name,' I said very slowly and clearly, making sure that she and everyone else on the train heard me.

She gave me an odd look but said no more. It was below her dignity to talk to a foreigner even though her country was being defeated.

I was very hungry and saw that the German woman had some apples. She saw me eyeing them and, despite her open hostility, reluctantly handed me one.

'Thank you very much,' I told her with a self-satisfied smile. I had to keep on eating and drinking to sustain myself, especially now when I was going to live and not die.

With my *P* now removed and placed in my pocket to be kept as a souvenir, I felt more and more free. Malach was sitting at my side, and I stroked her fur. The days of my double life were finally over, and I could proclaim my true identity to anyone and everyone with pride.

The train seemed to go too slowly for me. I was very impatient to reach my destination. I looked out the window and admired the beautiful scenery. There were many lovely trees and flowers growing all along. The sun was shining and I believed it was shining just for me.

Finally, the train jolted to a stop. Through the open window, I could see a sign post with 'Halle' written on it. Halle was a much bigger town than ours, and the station swarmed with tense and anxious-looking people. I was not surprised. Their great Fatherland was falling. Everyone was in a hurry, pushing and running in all directions. They were probably running away from Halle to a territory that Germany still held. But I knew that Germany could not last for much longer.

I took out my identity card and wondered what

Stefania Iwkiewicz would say if she could see me with her identical name. A smile came over my face. I was alive, and the war was nearly over. I began to imagine that I would eventually go home. A shiver inside me brought me back to reality. Home? No one waited there for me. Where was my home now?

I left the platform and began looking at the passers-by as if hoping to meet someone. I remembered that my permit was only for a one-way trip and became a little concerned that I should find overnight accommodation.

I made my way to the local police station, where an American-appointed German police officer was in charge. He asked me to sit down and show him my identity card.

After looking at my card, he said, 'I see that you're a Polish girl. You may soon be going home. How long have you been in Germany?'

'Two and a half years,' I told him.

'That's a long time,' he said. 'But not long enough to have picked up such good German. Why, you even look German.'

'I know,' I said. 'I have deceived many people with my looks and pretended to be someone else for two and a half years.'

'Well, what's your real name?'

'My name is Mala Szorer.'

'That name doesn't sound very Polish to me. I'll have to call my superintendent to listen to this. You may have committed crimes here.'

'Call your superintendent,' I told him. 'As far as I'm

concerned, you can call the whole world. I want all of you to know that the only crime I have committed is not admitting to the Nazi murderers that I am Jewish.'

The policeman's face suddenly took on a different expression. He smiled broadly, and his eyes widened in wonder. He even took off his hat.

He picked up the phone and quickly dialled a number.

'Gertrude,' he said. 'I have a very important visitor here. Come and take her home. See to it that she gets a good meal, and find out what she wants to do.'

When he had put down the phone, I said, 'Please, sir, I really came here to see if you could help me find some Jewish survivors. I was told by an American soldier in my town that there were some concentration camp survivors, right here in Halle.'

I did not know exactly what a concentration camp was and imagined that many people lived there together. 'It's a pity I did not know about them before,' I said. 'I would have tried to join them.'

'It was better that you did not know, my dear,' he replied grimly. 'As a German, I feel ashamed to tell you what happened to the people in those camps.'

Only then did I begin to understand what Frau Perlmutt had told me about those Jewish people from Leipzig. How they must have suffered! At the time, I had not wanted to know and must have appeared indifferent to Frau Perlmutt. Now, almost fifty years later, I feel the shame of my indifference, as false and as necessary as it was then.

How heartless Frau Perlmutt must have thought me.

But I had had no choice then. My heart had nearly stopped beating when she spoke to me that evening. It was only my natural acting ability that kept me from breaking down.

A very friendly woman soon entered the police station and introduced herself as Gertrude. She asked me to come to her home and offered to carry my suitcase.

I thanked her most kindly but would not allow her to carry my bag. It was clear to me that her husband was not a Nazi if he was now appointed to sit at the police station.

At home, Gertrude offered me some meat, but I said I preferred a slice of bread and butter and some coffee. She prepared for me a lovely dairy meal and sat down to eat with me. She was almost as friendly as Frau Ehrhardt had been.

'My husband said that I was to expect a very important visitor,' said Gertrude. 'Are you, by any chance, a relative of his?'

I laughed. 'No, I'm not his relative. I am Jewish.'

Gertrude's eyes filled with sadness. 'You poor child,' she said as she embraced me. She soon began to tell me a story with which I was already familiar.

'My husband and I and some members of our family were all on the blacklist because we did not join the Nazi party. Who knows what would have happened to us if our country had won the war?'

I then told her how Herr Perlmutt had been threatened by a young soldier when he stopped saying '*Heil Hitler*' in greeting. '*Wart einmal bis der Krieg verbei ist*,' he had said. 'Wait until the war is over.'

'You are mature for your age,' Gertrude said.

'I have had to fend for myself since I was twelve-and-a-half years old,' I told her. 'I had to be my own father and mother.'

'You poor child,' she murmured again.

At first, I could not take it all in fully. I remembered how the Germans had behaved in Poland. Gertrude had not lost her humanity. She was kind and soft-hearted, which greatly amazed me.

Soon Gertrude suggested that I stay with them for a little while. She showed me her beautiful, big garden. Seeing the perfectly kept lawn and flower beds, I was nearly tempted. Ever since I was a small child, I had loved flowers and grass, and here there were fruit trees as well, just like in my Uncle Abram's garden. Gertrude picked some blackberries and handed them to me.

Gertrude soon began telling me about her family, and I listened earnestly, showing great interest in what she was saying.

'There are three of us here,' Gertrude said. 'My husband and I and our son. The war is almost finished, and he is at home now. But our house is very large, and we can accommodate you, too.'

I had seen a picture of a young boy dressed in a military uniform in the lounge. He had no medals or ribbons, so I assumed that he had not distinguished himself in battle or done anything heroic, as most of his friends had.

He was a mere *Gerfreiter*, low on the military echelon. The soldiers at the hotel had sung a denigrating little verse about the *Gerfreitereren*. '*Gehen sie weiter, gehen sie weiter, sie sind ja nur Gerfreiter.* Go away, go away, you are only a private.' The song was supposed to have encouraged the soldiers to distinguish themselves in the battle. Gertrude's son had not succeeded in doing so and had, therefore, remained a private.

You are very kind,' I said to Gertrude, 'but I long to be reunited with my people. That's why I came to Halle, to meet up with some Jewish people, with concentration camp survivors. Do you know where I might be able to find some? I so much want to meet Jewish people again. Please help me find them, Gertrude.'

'Leave your suitcase here for a while, and come with me,' she said.

We left the house together and walked to an encampment surrounded by high, barbed-wire fences. Behind the fences was a large group of people. As we drew nearer, I noticed that they were emaciated and looked like living skeletons. They all resembled the Russian prisoners I had fed in the square. I saw no children or old people, and I understood that none had survived.

So these were the survivors of the concentration camps! Unbelievably, they were still guarded by Germans! However, these were not Nazi concentration camp guards but soldiers who had been appointed by the Americans. I imagined that the Jewish people were guarded to ensure that they would not try to take revenge on the local residents. The precaution seemed unnecessary to me for these poor souls had no more strength to do anything but sit and stare blankly, remembering what they had endured.

I longed to join them, but as much as I tried, I could not attract their attention. They turned away from me.

'Can anyone speak to me?' I shouted through the fence. 'I want to speak to someone because I am Jewish like you.'

I tried speaking in Yiddish, German, Polish and even a little Russian, but to no avail. They gesticulated at me to leave them alone. They must have believed I was a naughty German girl who had come to make fun of them. After all, I was well-dressed and looked well-fed, too. How could a Jewish girl look so healthy?

Deeply disappointed, I turned away and went back to Gertrude's house.

As kind as Gertrude was, I did not want to stay in a place where a member of the household had been in the German army until a few days earlier, even if he was only a *Gerfreiter*. I stood looking at the photograph of the young soldier, and a shiver went through my spine. I remembered how those soldiers back in Tarnogród shot that little boy in cold blood, and here was one dressed in the identical uniform.

'Our son never did anything more than necessary,' Gertrude said, reading my thoughts. 'He had good lessons from us. The army was compulsory for all the German boys, as you know. Torturing people was not his way, coming from a house like ours.'

He must have deserted, I thought. Otherwise, he would still be fighting because Berlin had not yet fallen.

But even if he was a deserter, I would not stay around

to meet him. I was still in Germany, and still afraid. And I was all alone in the world. He might have kept his gun; if he had decided to shoot me, not one person would have missed me. For a moment, I even imagined that Gertrude's husband had sent me to their house for the purpose of having me shot. But when I looked at Gertrude's kind eyes, I dismissed that thought. She had had the opportunity to harm me before now, but she had only been helpful to me.

After contemplating my next move for a while, I thanked Gertrude for her kindness and headed back to the police station to ask for a travel permit back to the hotel. I was not quite sure if the Perlmutts would take me back, and I felt humiliated to have to ask them, but I had no choice. For the time being, I had nowhere else to go.

'Can you issue me a travel permit to go back home?' I asked Gertrude's husband when I got back to the police station.

'So you've decided to go back, have you?' he asked in a concerned tone of voice. 'What will you do if the Perlmutts don't want you back?'

'Then I will just have to go to the American army and speak to that Czech soldier to see what he suggests.'

'I can see that your mind is quite made up,' he said. 'But I'm afraid I have no authority to issue you a travel permit. For that, you'll have to go to the American headquarters.'

He gave me directions.

'I am on duty here,' he said, 'or I would take you there myself. But you look like a girl who can find anything herself.'

'Yes,' I said. 'I can. Experience taught me to be independent.'

He wished me well in the future and bade me farewell.

BOOK FOUR

Return to Poland

28. Followed by Trouble

I made my way to the American headquarters, a house surrounded by a large group of tents hung with American flags. Several sentries stood outside, so I hesitated for a few minutes. But they looked quite benign, and I finally approached them.

They asked me questions in English and indicated that I should go away when I did not respond. In desperation, I drew a big *Magen David* on a piece of paper and held it high while pointing at myself. One of the soldiers soon understood and quickly went into the tent. After a few moments, he came out and indicated to me to follow him inside, staring at me all the time.

Appearing fearless, I followed him to the bedside of a much-decorated officer whose leg was heavily bandaged. I tried to speak to him in German, Polish and Yiddish, but he did not show any signs that he understood any of those languages. English must have been the only language he understood.

To my delight, he gave me a friendly smile and pointed to a chair next to his cot. I sat down and showed him the travel permit that I had used for this journey. He observed me with great curiosity, and after much gesturing, I succeeded in establishing that I needed another permit for the return journey. I duly received the required document, feeling quite proud of my success, not having spoken his language.

My pride dissipated when I remembered that I would be returning to the hotel. It was not the Perlmutts to whom I objected, for they alone had been kind to me. But the idea of going back and meeting the other workers filled me with dread and humiliation. I had come to hate the hotel, as it signified all the suffering I had endured during my time in Germany.

I also had to consider that as nice as the Perlmutts had been in the past they might not allow me to enter their hotel again. They might have little use for me now that the war was almost over. But after six years of the war, I would not let fear stop me. Especially not now, when I was a free person.

In any case, whether they welcomed me with warmth or turned me away, I had no choice but to make the attempt.

As I boarded the train to the hotel, sadness overwhelmed me, a feeling that persisted throughout my journey. I remembered my jubilation when I had left for Halle, remembered how good it had felt to regain my identity and proudly proclaim my name. Now, here I was, again having to use my identity card in the name of Stefania Iwkiewicz, for without it, I could not have travelled. When I had left for Halle, I had been filled with hope of meeting Jewish people. But I had not succeeded in meeting a single one, and that was my greatest disappointment.

The familiar streets and faces in the hotel did nothing

to ease my sorrow. Hoping to improve my mood, I decided to visit the Ehrhardts. I picked up Malach and walked quickly to their house.

They were delighted to see me, believing I had come to stay with them. We chatted for a while, and then I bid them a nice goodbye.

'I am going to pay a visit to the Perlmutts,' I told them. 'But I may be back.'

Should the Perlmutts decide that they had had enough of me, I would still have a place to go.

To my great relief, Herr and Frau Perlmutt welcomed me back as if I had been one of the family, even helping me with my suitcase. The staff, however, made their resentment of my return very obvious. Over tea, the Perlmutts apologised and asked me not to take any notice of them.

News of my true identity must have spread, for the next morning, a woman by the name of Frau Polter came to see me. After introducing herself, she said, 'Like you, I am Jewish. I would like you to meet my husband. He is not Jewish, but he is a fine man all the same.'

On the way to her house, I was very excited, for here, at last, I met a Jewish woman. Frau Polter told me that she had gone into hiding in a German friend's house when the Gestapo came to look for her. Her husband had been arrested and tortured but hadn't revealed her whereabouts. He had been in a concentration camp, she told me tearfully, and he had only come home a few days before.

The Polters were well off and suggested I live with

them; they were elderly and had no one to whom to leave their property when they died. I explained to them how much my Jewish heritage meant to me, especially after the experiences of the previous six years. Having seen the level of bestiality of another culture, I was more determined than ever to rediscover my people. I knew if I were to accept their generous offer, I would slowly but surely forfeit my Jewishness in exchange for material gain.

Herr and Frau Polter were deeply touched and thanked me for my explanation, saying that, as much as they would have liked me to have accepted their offer, they fully understood me and sincerely hoped I would be able to fulfil my aspirations.

'We are old, and we have lost everything,' they said. 'But you are young. Young people can still achieve the impossible.'

I visited the Polters every day during the rest of my stay with the Perlmutts. When I told them that I had decided to go back to Poland in the hope of finding some Jewish people there, Frau Polter gave me a pair of big diamond earrings, saying that they would keep me for a long time if the need arose. I did not really appreciate the value of the gift then, knowing nothing about diamonds. The only diamonds I wanted then were my lost family. Nevertheless, I put the earrings away in a safe place.

On May 8, we heard that the war had ended and that the Germans had surrendered. I did not show my co-workers that I rejoiced in their downfall. To have done that would have been wrong even though they had not shown me much kindness. And the Perlmutts were decent people. They did not deserve to see me gloating; they deserved my appreciation of their kindness. Had they refused to let me back in on my return from Halle, I would have been in a difficult situation, and I might have made an unwise decision. Now, because they had taken me back, I had the time to think things over carefully.

They did not expect me to work, and I walked through the streets of the town. I did not wander aimlessly; I walked around purposefully with the hope of meeting another Jewish–American soldier. Unfortunately, there did not appear to be any, or at least I did not recognise them. Since I could not speak English, I could not converse with the other American soldiers. But every time I saw one, I displayed the paper *Magen David* I had fashioned in Halle. They stared after me for a long time, perhaps wondering how a Jewish girl had found her way to this town. I could not explain anything to them because of the language barrier. But I could not resist smiling at the soldiers, at my liberators. That was a language they all understood, and they smiled back in understanding. I continued showing the *Magen David*, knowing that if there were a Jewish boy among them, they would tell him about me. Then he would come to see me, even if it would only have been out of curiosity.

The Polish workers began travelling back home to their parents.

'Don't forget to write your book when you get home, Stefania,' they all reminded me.

'I won't,' I said. 'And thanks for helping me improve my command of Polish.'

'Your parents will be very proud of you when you get home,' they said.

A great sadness suddenly enveloped me. I felt very disheartened, and the longing for all my dear ones became even more acute now. I imagined that they were all waiting for me at home. My dear mother would welcome me with a steaming bowl of soup and immediately compliment me on my maturity. 'Listen to how she speaks Polish,' she would say proudly. 'You are a writer? Who would have believed it? What a brave girl you were, Mala dear.' She would hold me in her arms for a long time. What a nice feeling that would be. 'Come to me,' my father would say, and he, too, would embrace me. How I would have loved to pour out my heart to them, as only a child can to parents.

With a sudden jolt, I emerged from my wonderful fantasy. I knew I had to get the dream out of my mind and accept that I was now all alone. It was crucial that my mind remained clear.

It did not take long before the neighbours of the Perlmutts began coming to the hotel to relate stories of how their Polish and Ukrainian workers had left with their employers' jewellery and other belongings.

'Is your Stefin still here?' I heard them ask the Perlmutts.

'Watch what she takes. Don't forget.'

I was not insulted or surprised by their comments. Polish workers stole shamelessly and with quite a bit of pride. They had even entered into an informal pact to steal all the valuables from their employers. When they invited me to join their pact, I refused, saying I was an honest girl, brought up by honest parents. They were not impressed and seemed to think I was foolish.

I was not in a particular hurry to travel to Poland, still hoping to find some Jewish people in Germany. However, my search was fruitless in our town, and I gave up the effort after a while.

I travelled to Leipzig, to visit the zoo for the last time. 'Goodbye, dear monkeys,' I said. 'I am free at last.' I laughed out loud and the people in the zoo must have believed I was crazy, but I did not care. It was better to be crazy than to be hunted like an animal. With pride in my heart, I stopped an old German lady and asked her, 'Can you tell me if there are any Jewish people still alive in Leipzig?'

'Jewish people?' she asked. 'Go to the *Gemeinde* at 10 Lehr Strasse; they may be able to help you there.'

She had obviously not been well informed as to what had happened to the Jews, believing that everything remained as it used to be. Nevertheless, I decided to go to that address and try my luck.

I soon found the building, but it was deserted except for a frightened old man, peering out of one of the upper windows. He did not answer me when I asked if there were any Jews inside. If he was Jewish himself, he was still afraid to tell me. He certainly looked Jewish to me and probably had no home yet, so he stayed in that sad building at 10 Lehr Strasse. Someone must have hidden him during the war, or he would not have been there now.

Disappointed, I went to the station and did not speak to anyone else on the way back to the Perlmutts. I had to think very carefully about my next step. If only Geena had still been in the hotel, I would have consulted her. I missed Geena, that gentle girl who knew my tragic story and was so sympathetic.

I had not yet confided in any of the Polish girls in the park that I was Jewish, as I was not sure of what their reaction would be. What would they say if I told them? Would they embrace me and rejoice at my survival? Maybe they would just be bewildered like my school friend Irena had been when I entered Tarnogród. 'Mala, you are still alive?' she had said. 'All the Jews have been killed.' I remembered how her father tried to hand me over to the Germans. No, I was not going to tell them yet. I would still pretend to be Stefania Iwkiewicz for quite a while more, for as long as I needed.

When I heard that the last Polish workers were leaving to return to their families, I joined them in a small party in the park, where we usually met.

'You come from the district of Lublin,' said a girl called Aniela Statjewska. 'Let's travel together.'

'That sounds like a good idea,' I said. 'But will you be able to put me up for a while as I don't really know yet where I am going?'

'I am afraid that won't be possible,' she replied.

I realised that I was once again on my own. The only difference was that I was now much older and better able to fend for myself.

I had no money, but I did have many dresses. And what's more, I had a lot of courage, which the six years of suffering could not take away from me; that was worth more than money.

I returned to the hotel to prepare myself to leave. On the spur of the moment, I called the Perlmutts to watch me pack, so they could be certain I took only my own belongings. I did not know yet what a wise move this was.

'Please,' I implored them. 'Go check that all your jewellery is intact before someone else takes it, and I am accused.'

'Where will you go from here?' asked the Perlmutts, knowing full well the difficulty of my situation.

As you already know,' I said, 'I am a big fighter. I am confident that I will find my place somewhere.'

After a while, Herr Perlmutt handed me three hundred marks. 'Unfortunately, they are not worth much these days,' he said apologetically, 'because the German money has been drastically devalued.'

I could not believe my good fortune and thanked him kindly.

'You have been a very good and diligent worker,' he said. He pressed an envelope into my hand. 'Here. You must take this letter also and show it to the porter at the railway station. It is vital that you do so.'

What could possibly be in it? I wondered. Little did I

know what an important letter he had given me and how helpful it would be.

I thanked Herr Perlmutt, and with a cheery goodbye to all of them, I set out on my journey, armed with a good command of the Polish language and quite a few belongings. My suitcase was full of lovely dresses that the kind dressmaker had made for me. On my way to the railway station, I went to say goodbye to her, but she was not in. She had left a note on her door which simply read: Gone Away. I was very puzzled. Why had she disappeared just when I was leaving? I wanted to thank her for her kindness and promise to keep in touch with her in the future, but she had mysteriously disappeared, as she had mysteriously appeared in the street one day to invite me up to her room.

While I stood there feeling sorry that I could not take proper leave of the dressmaker, I felt something rubbing against my ankles. Turning around, I saw that it was my dear friend Malach. I picked her up, and we headed off together. I was not alone.

I arrived at the station and handed Herr Perlmutt's envelope to the porter as instructed. He tore the seal and read the note carefully. Glancing at me kindly, he handed it back to me. 'A nice piece of paper you have here, Stefin,' he said. 'It is yours to keep. Now take in your suitcase and make yourself comfortable.'

I was quite certain that by now all the Germans in my town had heard that I was Jewish and was therefore very surprised at his kindness.

'The Perlmutts were always speaking very highly of you,' he said politely. 'You are a real lady, and your parents will be proud of you when they see you. Have a nice journey, dear.'

As I boarded the train, a group of Polish boys and girls began harassing me, and I wondered why.

'Don't you know you're not allowed to have any luggage with you?' they said sternly.

'Did the porter let you take it in? He didn't let us keep our bags with us. We all had to leave our luggage in the last compartment,' they said. I could not understand why I was the only one allowed to take my suitcase in with me.

They were all jealous of me, and I became quite frightened. I went back to the porter to see if perhaps he had made some mistake. He had made no mistake, he said. He was in charge, not they, and I was to ignore their questions.

Feeling somewhat relieved, I went back into the train with my suitcase and sat down to read the Perlmutts' letter.

Sie, Stefania, Mala Szorer, war mir eine treue und zuwerlesige Arbeiterin, und hat ihre Arbeit voll und ehrlich erfüllt. Ihr Gepäck ist ihr eigentum.

She, Stefania, Mala Szorer, was an honest and diligent worker, and carried out her work to our great satisfaction. Her luggage contains only her own property.

Signed: Herr Friedrich Perlmutt

I re-read the letter a few times and began to understand its significance. I remembered how the Perlmutts' neighbours had complained about their workers who had left with their employers' jewellery and other valuables. How glad I was now that I had asked the Perlmutts to watch me pack. That is why the Perlmutts had written that letter. Without it, I would not have been allowed to keep my belongings with me. I understood immediately that the luggage of the Polish boys and girls would not arrive in Poland. However, I would have mine. I would need it more than they needed theirs because they all had families to help them; I had no one and nothing but my dresses and belongings to barter for food and board.

The train began to move away from the familiar place at last, and everyone sang Polish songs. One of them was 'Mother wait for us, we are coming home to you at last.' I did not join in and wished I had at least one friend with whom to converse.

I looked out the window at the beautiful scenery and the colourful flowers. I made up a poem on a scrap of paper about how I missed my family more than ever now that I was free.

I looked up from my poem and suddenly saw Marysia coming towards me. Next to her was her husband and a boy I had never seen before.

'Stefciu!' Marysia said, 'This is my husband's cousin Michael. We have a long journey ahead of us and plenty of time for the two of you to talk.'

'Marysia dear, I am very busy writing,' I said to her. 'And I can only concentrate if I am alone, as you must understand.'

'You will have plenty of time to write when you get

home,' said Marysia's husband, looking for a place to sit. Luckily, the seat next to me was taken, but they positioned themselves directly opposite me, to my dismay.

I became very uncomfortable and rather concerned. I thought that they might have known all along that I was Jewish and kept it a secret from the Germans because Michael was hoping that I would marry him one day. They must have decided that in Poland they would be able to force me easily into marriage. Perhaps, they might even kidnap me.

At the beginning, I had befriended Marysia because she was not too clever, but now I began to wonder about the wisdom of the friendship. I was quite certain that Marysia genuinely did like me, but she also wanted to have me as her sister-in-law. I became restless, especially as I had not yet decided in which part of Poland to alight. I was only familiar with Tarnogród, a small town, and the surrounding villages, not the vast country called Poland.

There was no one to whom I could turn. I was afraid to confide in the others. They were hostile to me because the porter had allowed me to keep my suitcase with me. And I reminded myself that the boys had believed that I was too proud, for I had always refused to go out with them. They certainly would not help me now. I searched the faces of all the girls and decided not to trust any one of them either.

'Are you taking that cat back to Poland?' Marysia now asked.

'Yes,' I told her. 'I am.'

'I want to tell you a secret, Stefciu dear, but please do not be offended. You know how much I like and admire you. Some of our Polish friends believe that you are a little peculiar, that you like that cat better than boys. I regret to tell you, they make fun of you behind your back.'

Hearing this, I began to stroke Malach heartily and was fearful that her husband and his cousin might then decide to kill my cat back in Poland. But I doubted they would succeed for Malach appeared to be immortal.

'This cat belongs to our family,' I told Marysia. 'I was always the one who fed it, and I decided it was best to take her with me wherever I go.'

I had to try very hard to get rid of my new enemy without offending her in any way.

'Please forgive me,' I said. 'But I must continue writing.'

I wrote a few words and left the paper in full view for them to read. I began a letter to my mother, saying, 'Mother, I am coming home to you at last. Put on a great feast for me.'

Then I decided that as long as they thought me peculiar, I would act that way. I stood up and began dancing around the train, holding Malach like a dancing partner. They all thought that was funny and joined in, but I sat back down.

'You don't look very happy, Stefania dear,' someone said. 'Why don't you join in our conversations and songs? Aren't you excited at the thought of seeing your parents at last?'

'I have a headache,' I said.

'You must be over-excited,' they said. 'You didn't have a headache ever before.'

'Perhaps she needs glasses,' a boy suggested. 'Maybe she's ruined her eyes, writing all the time.' And he laughed loudly. They all joined in making fun of me.

Soon after, they began discussing the valuables they had taken from their employers. One girl whispered excitedly that half the things in her suitcase were not her own belongings.

'I took the lady's jewellery,' said a girl named Hanka. 'I wonder what they will say when they find out.'

'I did the same thing,' said another. 'I took only the best things. I have enough to give presents to my entire family and all my friends. How happy they will be to see me.'

They all laughed heartily and suddenly, one girl asked, 'What about you, Stefania? What did you take from the Perlmutts?'

'I took nothing,' I told them, 'because my family doesn't need anything. They have everything they want.'

'Did you hear that?' said a boy named Jurek. 'Her family has everything. What a rich family you have. After six years of war, they are not short of anything. Lucky devils.'

'You should still have taken a few things,' someone said. 'We worked for so many years without pay. They deserve to have their valuables taken.'

'You're right that they deserve it,' I told them. 'But my conscience does not allow me to steal.'

'You've always been different. You never even wanted to go out with boys. You only went out with Marysia and her husband. Don't you want to get married one day?'

I smiled but did not answer.

'Don't forget to send your book when you finish writing it,' they all said mockingly. Then they handed me their addresses.

'What is your address?' they wanted to know.

Each girl had made a friend and was going to get married. Everyone wanted to invite me to her wedding.

'Don't forget to invite us to yours,' they said. The only ones who looked unhappy were Marysia's husband and his cousin. Their stares frightened me, and I decided to get off the train before they did.

'I want to go to university first. I am still too young to settle down,' I said.

'What about your bad stepmother?' Marysia wanted to know.

'She died,' I told her.

We stopped not far from Kraków to use the conveniences and to stretch our legs.

'Look!' one boy suddenly exclaimed. 'Our train has been shortened. The luggage car must have been disconnected and left on German soil. Now we have nothing, not even our own belongings!'

They all became dejected, and one girl said, 'You're lucky, Stefania, you still have your suitcase, but your things are probably not worth much. Ours were worth a small fortune.'

'Yes, my things are not worth much,' I said, for I began to be fearful that they would try to take away some of my things out of jealousy.

No one made any move towards me. I was then afraid

that they might do this outside the train. I knew most of them were travelling beyond Lublin, so I had decided to stay in Kraków.

I stood at the station for quite a while, a lonely figure among strangers who were waiting to travel to different towns. I wondered what had become of my friend Malach, for I had not seen the cat on the train for the last hour or so. As usual, she had so mysteriously disappeared.

'*Przepraszam, Panienke*,' a voice suddenly said. 'Excuse me, young lady.'

Frightened, I turned around and saw a middle-aged man approaching me. He seemed to have come out of nowhere. Although he looked very kind, I was apprehensive and afraid to answer to this stranger.

'Are you waiting for someone?' he wanted to know.

'My aunt is supposed to have met me. I can't understand why she is not here. I am tired from the journey from Germany, and I would like to find a cheap and clean hotel for a night or two before finding my family in town.'

'I have a *dorożka*, a horse-drawn coach,' he said. 'If you want, you can stay with my wife and my daughter. We have a big house and take in young ladies as lodgers.'

I then told him that I would like to meet his wife first before committing myself to staying with them.

'That's no problem at all,' he said. 'Let's drive home, and you can meet my wife.'

'I have no money,' I said.

'We are very short of clothes right now. You can pay with a dress. Do you have any to spare?' he asked.

'I can only spare one dress, in return for a few days' accommodation,' I told him.

'That will be fine,' he said.

He next took me to his *dorożka*, and I looked on as he harnessed himself like a horse. I sat comfortably as he ran along, holding on to my precious suitcase and wondering where Malach was.

After a short ride, he pulled up in front of a very large house and asked me to follow him. I then told him that I would rather see his wife outside first, before entering his house. He soon brought her out, together with two of their lovely daughters. She introduced herself as Mrs Adamski and invited me in. I was assigned to a room which was occupied by two other girls who had also just returned from Germany.

Malach appeared a day later, and I spent the next few days walking through the streets of Kraków with her in search of Jewish faces. I visited cafés and parks and stood in the streets observing all the passers-by. I soon learned, after speaking to many Poles, that Poland was still as anti-Semitic as ever, if not more so.

One day, I was looking at a shop window and at the same time talking to a girl who tried to invite me into her home. I hesitated going with her because I was afraid of strangers and told her I could not come that day. 'I shall come and visit you another day,' I promised her.

She gave me her address and told me I was welcome any time.

I was happy that I had now made one friend and decided to visit her sometime soon. I did not know how very soon that would be because from afar I could suddenly see Marysia's cousin, Michael. He soon caught up with me and began talking to me.

'Remember me, Marysia's cousin?' he asked as he neared me. 'I saw you getting off in Kraków and decided to follow you. I have heard a lot about you and know that you are a very shy girl and a very bad mixer. Believe me, I have met many girls in Bitterfeld but was not interested in any of them.'

I did not say anything, so he went on.

'Perhaps my size frightens you, Stefania? I can't make myself smaller, but I can promise you that you will never be short of anything if you agree to marry me. My family has become very rich during the war, Stefciu, and I am the only son. How would you like to live in a beautiful house in Zamość?'

Heavens! I thought. He was our neighbour. Zamość was not far away from Tarnogród.

I was now more than certain that he had not the slightest inkling that I belonged to the Jewish people. He may have even believed that I had many relations here in Kraków and that perhaps I was coming to visit them before returning home. I fully realised that he must have known from Marysia that Krakow was not my home town.

'Please,' he began to implore me, 'can I take you out tonight to a cinema or restaurant? You choose, Stefciu.'

I realised it would not be too wise to show him that I was not in the least interested. Better to put him off for a while and wait for him to lose interest or wait until I could lose him in the vastness of Poland.

'I cannot come with you today,' I told him, looking at my watch. 'I already have an appointment, and I am expected within the hour.'

It was my good fortune that I still had the address which that girl had given me, and I asked directions from the first person who came along. Michael began to follow me and saw me enter that house. He took note of the address and decided that he was in no particular hurry, now that he knew where I lived.

After I saw him going away, I took leave from my new friend, telling her I would return the following day at ten o'clock in the morning. 'I have to go home now,' I told her. 'My mother is waiting for me.'

On the way, I rearranged my hair in a bun so that from afar I would look like a different person. I was fearful I would meet Michael on the way, but I did not.

When I entered the Adamskis' house, I told them that a boy was after me and should he manage to catch up with me, could they kindly tell him that I had left. I never went to see that girl again and was quite fearful of meeting Michael once more. I also decided to stay for a while and give Michael a chance to leave Krakow first.

After a week and a half, I settled my account with Mrs Adamski with an old cardigan and a dress, worth a small fortune in Poland in those days, and decided to travel on to Lublin. I packed my luggage and asked Mr Adamski to give me a lift back to the station in his *dorożka*.

Arriving in Lublin, I wondered if there were any Jewish people left. I had had some relatives there before the war and hoped to find some. I also hoped that perhaps I would meet some kind Pole who would feel sorry for me and would offer to keep me for a while. I fully realised what a difficult situation I was in, especially being a girl, but to my delight, hope was still with me, as usual.

Where to begin the search I did not yet know. Malach was once again near me, but she left all the thinking to me.

29. The Soldier Sanford

The sun was shining brightly, and I sat down on my suit-case to take a much needed rest. I could not, in any case, have walked very far with my luggage, nor did I know what my destination would be. After vacillating for a while as to which direction to take, I decided to stay put for a little while longer in case I would meet someone like Mr Adamski. I stood for quite a while in the fore-court of the station as if waiting for someone.

After a few minutes, I noticed a Polish soldier walking towards me. I watched him as he approached and thought that he looked Jewish. I was still very apprehen-sive and decided not to question him at all; instead, I would begin an innocent conversation.

Turning to him, I said sheepishly, 'I have just returned from Germany, and my parents are not here to meet me.'

'There's not much that I can do to help you,' he said. 'But I can direct you to the police station, if you wish. They might be able to help you. There are many new-comers in town.'

'Where did you come from?' I asked him innocently.

'I was in Russia for a while,' he said, 'and then in the army, fighting the Germans.'

'Did you manage to kill many of them?' I suddenly asked.

'Not as many as I would have wanted to,' he said. 'What funny questions for a young girl like you! What difference does that make to you, anyway? You look well fed and clothed. You could not have suffered like my . . .'

He let his voice trail off, but I knew he had been about to say 'my people'. And I now had no doubt that he was Jewish.

'What is the name of your town?' he asked in a friendly manner.

'I come from Tarnogród,' I told him, hesitantly.

'I've heard of Tarnogród,' he said, 'but what were you doing in Germany?'

'I volunteered for a labour exchange,' I told him.

'You must have been pretty unhappy at home to have wanted to leave at such an early age.'

'I had to leave Poland,' I told him.

He was observing me now with interest as though he had begun to suspect that I was not telling him the whole truth.

'You look and sound more German than Polish to me.'

'I can speak German very well,' I told him, 'but I am not German. Nor do I ever want to belong to that people.'

'They certainly looked after you well during your stay there. You are well dressed for a young girl, and you look well fed.'

I could see him trying to figure out who I really was.

'Are you sure someone will come to meet you?' he suddenly asked. 'Tarnogród is far from Lublin. Perhaps you should travel to Zamość first? That's closer to Tarnogród.'

Michael had mentioned a house in Zamość, and I quickly told the soldier that I was not interested in travelling there, as I had no relations there.

'That is quite understandable,' he said. 'It is not safe for a young girl like you to travel on her own unless it is absolutely necessary. You do, however, look to me as though you are quite capable of looking after yourself. I had a sister your age, and she could never have travelled on her own like you do.'

'What happened to her?' I asked, noticing he had spoken of her in the past tense.

He hesitated and then said, 'She's no longer alive.'

'What about the other members of your family?' I asked. He pretended not to hear me and ignored my question. He looked at me sternly and then said, 'Come along with me and have a bite in a café. You can tell me all about yourself while we eat.'

I followed him to a restaurant. It was filled with many soldiers who seemed to know him. We soon found empty seats, and I began to look around. Suddenly, I froze, for at a nearby table sat Michael. He must have followed me, and I had to do something quickly. I had to have protection.

I was now compelled to tell this soldier that a dangerous boy was following me and wished me harm. I indicated that Michael was in the restaurant and described him.

'We shall soon put an end to this,' he said.

He approached a group of his uniformed friends and asked them to join us at our table and pretend they were all my friends, too. Michael would not bother me in the face of such a risk.

The plan worked very well, and Michael suddenly got up to leave. But before he went out the door, he gave me an antagonistic look that said, 'I will find you at a time when you will not be surrounded by so many soldiers with their guns!'

The other soldiers soon left us for their own table, and we ordered food. I asked for some bread with butter and a coffee. I realised that the soldier did not order anything that was not kosher either.

'What is your name?' he asked me.

I did not answer immediately.

'Are you afraid to tell me your name?' he said.

'I am Stefania Iwkiewicz now, but I used to be called Mala Szorer,' I told him and wondered about my wisdom. Supposing I had made a mistake, and he suddenly became very unfriendly to me. Where would I go then, with Michael still lurking about?

I stroked Malach for reassurance, and the soldier asked, 'Why are you travelling with a cat?'

'This cat is my best friend. I call her Malach.'

The soldier's eyes widened in disbelief as I pronounced my cat's name. For a good few minutes he was quite unable to speak. 'Heaven, it's true!' he said. 'Malach is Hebrew for angel. You are a Jewish girl.'

I nodded, and he continued speaking excitedly. 'I can just about imagine what you have been through. Are you the only survivor of your family? I am not at all surprised that you survived as a Christian girl. You really do look like one. It's only when you mentioned your cat's name that I knew for certain you were Jewish. I'm also Jewish. I know Tarnogród because my Auntie Chaya married a teacher in that town. It was her second marriage. Her husband's name was Yanchi Akst.'

Although I had suspected from the start that he was Jewish, I could not believe that I heard him correctly. 'Yanchi Akst? Yanchi Akst was my maternal grandfather! What's your name?'

'Sanford,' he said. 'Come on, let's go. Let me take you to the *yeshivah*. There is someone there who will help you. You'll be safe from that Polish boy.'

'He is Ukrainian,' I told him. 'He says his parents made a lot of money during the war.'

'I quite believe him,' he said. 'But don't worry. We soldiers will scare him off for good!'

As we walked towards the *yeshivah*, I realised that this was another miracle and started to thank *Hashem* for saving my life once more – this time from the Ukrainian. I still could not fully comprehend why *Hashem* had chosen me out of my whole family to survive. My parents, my brother and my sisters had been far better people than I was. Why was I made fearless? Why was I given such a lot of courage and the strength to withstand all the suffering? Why had I survived?

But others had survived and experienced miracles. Anyone who survived the Holocaust survived with miracles. Perhaps one day I would read about them and find an answer. Perhaps I could begin to digest the trauma of the past six years and thus begin to think of the future.

Mr Sanford's family had also perished, though he did not know exactly how. He had survived because he had been a Polish soldier. 'We're lucky we're so young,' Mr Sanford said. 'So many people have lost their children, and they alone survived. For them there is no beginning. But we can build our lives and still be very happy.'

I asked Mr Sanford if he thought it was advisable for me to travel to Tarnogród, my home town, as I longed to see it once more.

He told me not to go anywhere near that place. 'If your house was not razed to the ground together with the rest of the ghetto,' he said, 'then I'm certain that there are Poles living there now.'

He told me terrible tales of partisans who returned to their houses after years of a perilous existence in the forests of Poland, only to be murdered by the illegal occupants. I could not understand how the Poles would behave like their oppressors. Instead of murdering people out of greed, they should have rejoiced that the Germans had not won the war. Little did they know that they were only 'Polish worms' in the eyes of the Germans, good only for betraying Jews.

30. The Yeshivah

Walking along, Mr Sanford asked, 'Where did you get such a nice dress with the war and all?'

'I have quite a few nice dresses in my suitcase,' I said.

He offered to help me sell some in the local market, saying that the money I would receive would keep me going for quite a while.

'You must have been joking when you said that you are taking me to the *yeshivah*,' I said. 'I am a girl, and only boys go to *yeshivah*.'

'The *yeshivah* now serves as a dormitory for Jews returning from Russia or from the forests,' he said. 'I am not sure that you'll have a bed or a blanket. But it's summer now, and the nights are warm. I trust in *Hashem* that our lot will improve before winter comes. In the meantime, you'll be among friends.'

We had reached the *yeshivah*, and Mr Sanford now prepared to depart, saying he had free accommodation and food in the Polish army. He would return in a few days to help me sell some dresses.

All alone once again, I said to Malach, 'It does look as though I will still need you for a while. So please don't leave me yet.'

On entering the *yeshivah*, I was shocked to see so many

demoralised people. They were dressed in tatters and looked as if they had endured much suffering. They told me some stories, and I listened fearfully.

Although the conditions in the *yeshivah* were not to my liking, I was happy to mix with friends without any fear of being Jewish. I related to all of them a little of my sufferings and my loneliness and soon fell asleep from exhaustion. I slept well, infused with a feeling of lightness and freedom in my heart that I had not experienced for a long time.

When I awoke, I was very happy because I saw that I was among good friends. They were all much older than I and did not let me do a thing. They prepared a meal for me and told me about themselves as I ate. Most of them had been married and had lost some members of their families. Some had been partisans who tried to return to their homes, only to find them occupied by Poles. Fearful of being murdered, they did not try to reclaim their houses.

The next day, Mr Sanford arrived and helped me sell one of my nice dresses in the market, as he had promised to do. The dress fetched quite a good price, sufficient to buy provisions for myself for a few weeks. I told him that I would really like to live with young girls, as the people in the *yeshivah* were much older than I was.

He made inquiries for me and found that Będzin had a large shelter for girls who had survived the concentration camps. He warned me, however, that some of the girls were a little demoralised from their experiences and that I might find them distressing. But when he informed me that orphaned children were being prepared for settlement in Palestine, I decided to set off without any delay. I was overjoyed and could not believe my good fortune. I was going to go to the spiritual home of my people.

31. The Girls in Dom Mondziejowski

I went straight to the shelter when I arrived in Będzin. When I entered the Dom Mondziejowski shelter, I was greatly saddened by the sight that met my eyes, for the girls there looked more dead than alive. They were emaciated, their skin was a greyish-white colour, and their eyes were hollow. Like the concentration camp survivors in Halle, they thought that I was a Christian girl who had come to look at them and have some fun at the expense of the survivors.

When I asked them if there was any room for me in the shelter, they stared at me, bewildered; why would a well-fed Christian girl want to join a group of emaciated girls in a house which resembled a hospital?

They looked at me in fear, as though I were mad. 'Why don't you stay with your parents?' they asked. 'This is a temporary home for Jewish girls.'

'My parents are dead,' I said. 'And I have no home. I'm also a survivor of the Holocaust, and I'm glad to have found you.'

They stared at me with disbelief for a long time and finally allowed me to embrace them. I promised them that I would look after them until their hair would grow a little, for I could see that they were too embarrassed to go out into the streets because of their baldness. Their hair had been shaved off in the camps, and they were all struggling with the effects of malnutrition and a variety of other illnesses.

Some of them were typhoid victims and were isolated from the other girls. They had no one to look after them as the Joint Israel Appeal found it difficult to get volunteers. I offered my services and was immediately taken on. I was careful not to use their facilities, and miraculously, I did not contract the disease. They all blessed me every time I fed them. Somehow, they recovered, a miracle indeed, for the Germans had not fed them for a long time.

'You are just like an angel sent from Heaven,' they all told me.

'I am not an angel,' I said. 'I am only a specialist in feeding people.'

I was happy that at long last I was among my own people, but even happier that *Hashem* had sent me to them on time, for they all needed my help. But I could see they did not really trust me. Every *Shabbos*, when the girls discussed their plans to emigrate to *Eretz Yisrael*, I was asked to leave the room because some thought that I had come to spy on them. The hostel manager and his wife tried to soothe my hurt feelings and asked me to forgive the girls, praising me in particular for my dedication to the typhoid victims.

It wasn't until *Rosh Hashanah* that they finally trusted me. We all went to a *minyan*, and the girls were surprised that I not only knew how to *daven* but that my knowledge of the *tefillos* and their place in the *siddurim* was superior to theirs. I had not seen a *siddur* for years, but I remembered everything.

32. The Final Escape

Our lives were still in danger because of the many anti-Semitic assaults taking place in Będzin. It was not even safe to walk the streets. Despite my experiences over the previous six years, I was unprepared for the murders and acts of violence that occurred daily in post-war Poland. Sometimes, I wondered if the war was really over. For those murderers killing was not a sin as long as they could hold on to the things that did not really belong to them.

I befriended two girls, Bella and Reginka, with whom I would talk about the conditions in Poland. One day, Bella told me that she, Reginka and ten other people had paid a Polish man to take them across the border to Czechoslovakia. They explained that Jewish people enjoyed more freedom there, and she asked me if I would be willing to join them.

I did not have to think about it too long before agreeing. Nor did much time elapse before Bella's father, another survivor of the Holocaust, took me aside for a private chat. He confided in me that he had hidden the family jewellery before being deported to Auschwitz. Luckily, he had found the cache on his return, and now he asked if I would take it across the border and deliver it to his needy relatives. At first, I objected, wondering why he did not ask his own daughter to smuggle the jewellery. Then I understood that acting as courier was the price of leaving Poland. Though a great risk was involved, my eagerness to get out of Poland was immense; I decided to take the chance.

Bella's father handed me a small parcel just before we arrived at the railway station near the Czech border. He instructed me to hide it on my body and explained that we would be searched before crossing. I was to run across before that happened, run as fast as my legs could carry me. He said I had a better chance than Bella or Reginka and even the ten men since I was then the strongest. At the last minute, I became frightened and questioned my wisdom at agreeing to the plan, but it was too late to change my mind. Anyway, it was my only chance to leave Poland.

As we approached the border, a Polish soldier tried to search me. However, I struggled with him and broke free of his grasp, then dashed across the border with bullets whistling past my ears. Luckily, I managed to reach the Czech side and hide under a train. The others were searched and allowed to cross.

When they all came across, I came out from hiding and boarded the train with them. I felt very tired after this ordeal and was glad to lie down on a bench and have a good rest. I had come close to being shot or captured and imprisoned in Siberia, perhaps for the rest of my life. *Hashem* had helped me once more, and I thanked Him for saving my life again, this time from armed border guards. When I heard a soft thud, I realised I also had to thank Him for saving Malach who now sat right beside me.

We soon travelled to Prague, where quite a few Jewish refugees were living. Reginka, Bella and I found accommodation in a convent, where friendly nuns cooked vegetarian meals for us. The three of us were shown to a bright, clean room. The men managed to find accommodation nearby, and they met us the following day to tour the town.

Walking along the streets of the city was a fine treat; the city was not only beautiful, but its people were also friendly, so different from the mean-spirited Poles across the border. They smiled when they saw us, as if to welcome us to their country. If we asked them for directions, they took us by the hand to show us the way. They knew we were Jewish and wanted to help us. They directed us to the famous Altneuschul synagogue with its Hebrew alphabet clock, but we could not go inside. We walked through the clean streets, looking at the impressive architecture. Now that we were in a friendly country, I breathed freedom and was grateful to be alive.

There was no point in remaining in Prague for long, and the adults in our group decided that it would be best to travel to Munich. According to some people with whom they had talked, there was a better chance of emigrating from Munich than from Prague. However, we needed travel permits, and we had no possibility of obtaining them. It would have taken weeks to obtain permits, and it was pointless even to attempt to get them without money. Enterprising as ever, the adults managed to get us on a train to Munich. During the journey, we hid beneath a great pile of coal in the engine room.

By the time we arrived in Munich, we looked as black as the coal, and I wondered how we were going to walk through the streets in that condition. The men, however, had the foresight to prepare some wet towels before our departure. We could at least clean our faces and hands if not our clothes.

We were directed to a museum that was being used as a temporary shelter and hospital for concentration camp survivors. Volunteers from the United Nations Relief and Rehabilitation Administration (UNRRA) cared for those survivors still too sick to travel. Those survivors were just like all others, starved and disease-ridden, near death at the time of their liberation. There were hundreds of people in this dismal condition. Even the children had little energy to run around.

I sat next to a woman who began to tell me that all four of her children were dead. She was quite certain that her husband had survived because he was a strong man and able to look after himself in normal times. But she did not know where he was or how to find him.

As she talked to me, an American soldier entered the museum and began looking at every patient. Suddenly, the woman stared at the soldier and began shouting, 'Leibel! Leibel!' at the top of her voice, before she fainted from her exertions. He was none other than her own husband who had managed to escape and join the American army. Their bittersweet reunion will remain in my memory forever: husband and wife in ecstasy at finding one another, in agony that their children had perished.

BOOK FIVE

A New Life

33. Journey to England

We, the healthy ones, were at first assigned to a place called Feldafing, which had been a well-known beauty spot and holiday resort before the war. The formerly elegant accommodations now resembled army barracks; each room contained rows and rows of cots, covered with black or dark grey blankets. But the rooms were neat and clean.

There was a lake nearby, and I spent some lovely times splashing in the water with the other girls. None of us could swim because most of the youngsters had spent their childhoods in concentration camps making bullets for the German army. We had no swimsuits either, but no one seemed to mind dunking into the cool water wearing skirts and dresses. In the evenings, we would gather around the cots and stay up half the night listening to each other's stories. Every survivor had a horrendous story to tell. When I related my story, they said, 'Yours is not a story to tell but to write.' I resolved to do so, knowing quite well that it would still take a long time before I would eventually publish my book. I was an inexperienced writer without very much education.

One night, we heard a big commotion from the men's dormitory, and all of us dressed and went to investigate. What I saw next made me shudder. There, in the middle of the room, lay a man who had been stabbed repeatedly.

He was conscious and pleading for help. No one came near him; he was dying slowly. He had been a camp guard who had tortured many people daily. After the liberation, he had hidden among the concentration camp survivors, safe until someone recognised him. I stood there and almost wished I could have inflicted one wound for every member of my family.

Soon the American authorities, fearing more revenge killings, had our camp, for that is what we soon called it, closely guarded by none other than German soldiers. Although they were now powerless to do anything to us survivors, they were constant reminders of what the Germans were capable of doing when in power. There was nothing we could do about the guards. They were there at the instructions of General Eisenhower, and he was in charge of the American army.

Because our barracks were crowded, the committee in charge decided to separate the younger girls and move them to Föhrenwald, another holiday resort. I was assigned to this group. Föhrenwald was not such a picturesque beauty spot as Feldafing. We had no idea that it had been used as a concentration camp. We missed the mature company of the older survivors. However, we realised there would now be a more cheerful atmosphere as many of the older people had lost children during the war and spent their time crying bitterly. Not having anything else to do, we just spent the days eating, cleaning our rooms and going for long walks. We all longed either to continue our studies or to train for some sort of profession. This opportunity did not come until much later.

There was no shortage of artistic talent among the youngsters in Föhrenwald, and we decided to put on a show in Munich. We wanted to cheer up the sick refugees living at the museum. One of the requirements for joining the performing group was a good voice since we not only had to dance but sing as well. How disappointed I was when I was told that my voice was not good enough to join the performers. I had to join the spectators instead. Little did I know then that if my voice had been good enough to join the performers, I would not be writing this story today.

Our mood was festive as we got onto the trucks to Munich, and we sang all the way there. This was to be a very joyous occasion for those youngsters. We were going to perform in freedom, for free people.

My talented companions put on a magnificent show, and everyone applauded at the end. After refreshments, two trucks arrived to take us back to Föhrenwald. All the performers now shared a kind of 'brothers-in-arms' spirit and piled into one truck; I rode with the remaining spectators in another. Our truck moved out first, and it was only when we reached Föhrenwald that we found out that the truck behind us had overturned on the way. The driver had been drunk, and he had lost control of the vehicle. The truck had skidded off the road into a ditch, killing everyone on board.

We were all speechless, and we cried for a very long time. It was difficult for us to believe that after surviving so many years of torture and starvation in concentration camps, those youngsters died in freedom. The sight of the bodies being brought back to Föhrenwald the following day was one of the saddest moments of all those traumatic years. For the first time, I could understand why *Hashem* had chosen not to give me a good voice.

One day, there was much excitement in our camp as General Eisenhower paid us a visit. He gave a speech and told us how much he admired our fortitude. He thought we had shown at least as much courage as his soldiers had on the battlefield. We felt very proud and presented him with a picture painted by a survivor. He also told us that efforts were being made to make our lives more comfortable and that he was personally involved in that operation.

I heard about his speech afterwards, for I was in bed with a headache at the time. Later, as he inspected the bedrooms, he personally gave me a bar of chocolate. I really only had a little headache, but I was very annoyed to see all those German guards, and I secretly blamed General Eisenhower for that. I did, however, enjoy his bar of chocolate; it had been six years since I last had such a luxurious treat.

The tranquil surroundings seemed to invite long walks and reflection, and I often wandered off alone. On those long, lonely walks, I would think about my remaining relatives. I had two uncles who used to visit us in Tarnogród from time to time all those years ago. As far as I knew, my father's two brothers were still living in Uruguay. My mother's brother had emigrated to Palestine when I was just a little girl and probably still lived there. I did not know his address, but I wrote a letter to him all the same.

Dear Uncle Shmuel,

I am not sure whether you will remember me, so let me introduce myself. I am Mala, the daughter of Itzik and of Frimchy, your late sister. You may recall your visit to us in Tarnogród in 1933 just before you left for Palestine. You played with me, and I complained about your prickly beard when you cuddled me. I also remember accompanying you with the rest of my family when you departed for your trip. I wanted to join you on your trip. How sorry I felt to see you leave. I still remember the large pineapple you brought us; we had never had pineapple before, and we saved it to celebrate the new addition to our house. All those happenings are engraved in my memory as if they only took place yesterday.

I so much regret having to be the bearer of such terrible tidings, but I am sorry to tell you that I am the only survivor of our whole family, including your father and your brother Abram. They and the whole family perished on November 1, 1942. I am the only survivor of the entire Jewish population of Tarnogród, as far as I know. You may consider me lucky, but I feel desperately lonely now. Please forgive the smudges on the paper, but it is my third attempt to write this letter without crying. If I were even to try a hundred times over, I could not staunch the bitter tears falling from my eyes. It is unlikely that you will ever receive this letter, since I haven't got your address, but expressing the bitterness on paper makes my big burden easier to bear. Keep well, and please forgive me for making you so sad.

Love, Mala

I addressed it to Shmuel Akst, Palestine. After finishing the letter, I felt better, for I had released a tiny amount of my sadness. And the very heavy obligation to provide evidence about what had happened to my people had been removed from my heart. I did not really expect that my uncle would receive it, and there was no point in waiting for a reply.

What happened next is as follows: When my letter arrived in Palestine someone read it and, touched by its content, placed a prominent advertisement in several newspapers. Before long, the news of my survival reached my uncle Shmuel. However, by the time his reply reached Föhrenwald I had already left, and the letter was returned to Palestine. Since the fatal truck accident on the way back from Munich had been reported in the media in Palestine, my uncle believed I had been among the casualties. He and his family mourned my 'death', especially saddened by the fact that I should have such an end after surviving hell on earth.

We were given the opportunity to register to a country of our choice. I registered to travel to Palestine, where I hoped to find my uncle. However, time passed, and my papers for Palestine did not arrive. Eager to get out of Germany as quickly as I could, I applied for a travel permit to England along with a group of teenagers and small children. Soon, I heard the good news from UNRRA that my application was approved. The British government had agreed to accept a quota of young refugees who wanted to complete their education in Great Britain. This suited me well since I still had a craving to further my own learning.

The excitement we all felt and the eagerness to leave

the country where we were so badly treated is indescribable. We counted the days and then the hours until the time of our departure arrived.

The day before we left, the ladies of the UNRRA organisation took us on a trip to the idyllic surroundings of the former Polish mountain resort of Garmiszcz. We spent the day learning patriotic English songs. I will never forget the thrill I felt at the thought of going to a country where being Jewish was not a crime. We were all very excited and spent the night practising our English songs.

At last, our great day arrived, and on October 30, 1945, we left Germany for England. The plane developed a mechanical fault, and we were forced to land at some unknown spot. How disappointed we all were when we discovered we were still in Germany. There were no hotels in the vicinity, and the only place we could stay that night was a deserted prison. It was a foul-smelling, filthy place, infested with lice and bed bugs. We spent the entire night scratching ourselves, the UNRRA ladies included. In the morning, we were told to shower and change all our clothes.

On November 1, 1945, we touched down in England and were taken to London. As the train pulled into the station, the UNRRA ladies prompted us to sing the English songs we had learned in Germany, especially the national anthem. The people in the station were very impressed by how well we sang them, and they applauded us. Our arrival must have been reported in the media, and many friendly people cheered us on, Jewish and gentile alike.

Although it was late morning, London was so enshrouded in thick fog that it looked as if it were the middle of the night. When the children saw the thick fog, they started screaming and rushed back onto the train. To them, the fog looked like the smoke from the crematoria of the camps, and they believed they had been brought to London to be gassed. It took some time for the UNRRA ladies to coax them back off the train and to explain to those frightened children that this was a perfectly natural phenomenon in London. I, too, had never seen a fog like that before.

Soon, we were all served sandwiches and oranges. Some children had not had fruit for six years. They had no idea what the orange 'balls' were and began tossing them around. But I remembered getting a finger or two of orange occasionally in Tarnogród when I was still a child. Sometimes, my Uncle Shmuel would send a parcel of citrus fruit from Palestine.

After the fog had lifted, we travelled to a temporary absorption centre for refugees called Wintershill Hall. There, we were taken care of by volunteers whose job it was to acclimatise us to a normal way of life. A few weeks later, I was placed with a group of girls assigned to Great Chesterfield, not far from Cambridge, to join other youngsters in an orphanage.

We were met in Great Chesterfield by Mr Wreshner, the principal of the orphanage, and by his wife. Almost immediately, he began to teach us English. Some of the pronunciation seemed impossible, especially the *th* sound. Mr Wreshner, however, had a trick for helping us form the sound: he told us to imagine that we had a hot potato in our mouth. He also gave each of us a mirror to watch ourselves as we attempted the pronunciation. I must admit that to begin with I thought that I would never master that strange language, but before long, I was quite proficient at it.

Our presence at the orphanage was reported in the press, and many people had now heard about us. Soon, we began receiving invitations to stay with families in London. The purpose was not only to extend a kindness, but also to reacquaint us with a normal way of life. That was something we had not experienced in over six years.

My first invitation was to a family called Stein who lived in the West End, somewhere near Oxford Street. I was very impressed with the welcome I received on my arrival. After talking for a few hours, Mrs Stein took me out shopping. She bought dresses and skirts and blouses and other necessities. By the time we returned from our shopping spree, Mr Stein had come home from work.

The Steins made a big fuss over me and asked me dozens of questions over dinner. Their questions did not annoy me; they asked in a way that made me feel they really cared about me, as though I were a member of the family. The feeling brought with it memories of home, though the Steins' modern house did not resemble our simple one in Tarnogród.

After supper, they invited some friends and introduced me to them. Although it was nice to meet their friends, I was grateful when they left and when Mrs Stein showed me to the bedroom. I was tired from the journey to the West End and from the shopping expedition.

My bedroom was lovely, with the carpets, curtains and bedspreads all of the same fabric. After having a bath, I realised that the pyjamas Mrs Stein had bought also matched the linen on the bed. Before getting into bed, I allowed myself to open the wardrobe and look at all the dresses Mrs Stein had purchased for me.

Just as I was getting into bed, Mrs Stein knocked on my door and came in. She sat on a chair next to me and began to speak, choosing her words carefully.

'I don't know how to begin, dear Mala,' she said. 'So I'll come straight to the point. My husband and I have not been blessed with children, and we would like to adopt you, if you would be willing to accept us as your parents. We know that we cannot possibly replace your own parents, but we feel that we can make you very happy. And materially, you will not be short of anything. You would make us very happy, Mala. What do you say to that?'

I looked at kind Mrs Stein and thought of her gentle husband who had tried very hard to cheer me up. Although I had known them for only one day, I was so fond of them that I asked Mrs Stein to give me until the following day to decide. She embraced me warmly, as if I were already her daughter, and bid me good night.

Mrs Stein had taken me by surprise. I must admit, I did not fall asleep at all that night. I lay in bed thinking of my dear parents. By morning, I had made my decision. Though my dear parents were no longer alive, I felt that I still belonged to them and that no one could ever replace them.

When Mrs Stein brought me a drink in the morning, she could see that I had been crying, so she was well prepared for my answer.

'It is much too soon for me to think about being adopted,' I told her. 'Those terrible events that happened all those years ago still seem to me as if they happened only yesterday.' And I very gently declined her kind offer, giving up the chance of living in a lovely home and having a loving family.

When we parted, we all had tears in our eyes. I cried on the train on the way back to the hostel. Yet I was quite sure that I had made the right decision. Even if I had not been reluctant to belong to a new set of parents, the Steins were not as observant as my parents had been and as I wanted to be.

Mrs Stein had packed all the clothing she had bought for me; I cried the whole way back to the orphanage and continued to cry while unpacking the beautiful clothes.

34. Finding Relatives

Before long, I was again invited to London, this time by the Rabinowitzes, a kind family from Cricklewood. Like the Steins, they welcomed me as if they had known me for a long time. When I first saw them, I felt a sense of familiarity, as if I had indeed known them.

Then I realised that Mr Rabinowitz resembled my late father. Perhaps the resemblance was my imagination playing tricks on me: Mr Rabinowitz was the first bearded Jewish man I had seen since I last saw my own father.

The Rabinowitzes were a sociable couple, and on *Shabbos* I went visiting with them. Their friends were eager to hear what had happened to me and to their families who had also lived in Europe. When I related to them the tragic events of the previous six years, I saw that they found it difficult to comprehend what I was telling them. But they all hugged me and told me not to cry, while doing so themselves.

'How could you have endured all that suffering and stayed so cheerful?' they wanted to know.

'I had a cat, for I was not worthy of seeing an angel,' I said, and they all looked at me perplexed.

Mr Rabinowitz, a *talmid chacham*, Torah scholar, gently helped me out. 'Retaining one's optimism is a special gift from *Hashem*.'

After breakfast Sunday morning, Mr Rabinowitz sug-gested that I go with him to see his shop, and we set off in his car.

The Rabinowitzes had four little children, and I thought it odd that he had not brought them along. 'Isn't anyone else coming?' I asked.

'No, not this time,' he replied.

We soon arrived at his shop. Mr Rabinowitz seemed to be in a hurry, and I could see that his purpose was not to show me their shop. There was another reason for taking me out alone. Mr Rabinowitz wanted to talk to me in private, without his children around to hear him.

'Look, Mala,' he said. 'My wife and I invited you here so that you could see what a normal family life is like. But in the three days you have been with us, we have come to know you and to like you very much.' He paused a moment before continuing. 'We would like you to live with us and become part of the family as our adopted daughter. What do you have to say to that?'

He went on without waiting for me to respond.

'Have you seen our twins Tosia and Marysia? They're also adopted, and they are very happy with us. When the time comes, we will marry them off and provide them with everything they need, as if they were our nat-ural born children. We want to do the same for you, Mala.'

'This is the third time I have been asked if I would like to be adopted,' I said. 'Please do not be cross with me. I had such sweet parents and cannot accept anyone else in their place. It still hurts me so much to think that they are not here any more. I want to keep on dreaming and imagining that they are still alive.'

His eyes filled with tears, but like the Steins, Mr Rabinowitz understood me. The following day, I returned to Great Chesterfield, feeling as if I were leaving my own relatives behind. I began to question my wisdom and the logic for refusing and continuing to live in hostels and orphanages. But my refusal arose from an emotional dictate, not from logic.

Some time later, the Jewish refugee committee arranged for our group of girls to go to a hostel at Kings Langley near Watford. A charitable gentleman had put a large house there at the committee's disposal. A few days after we had settled into our new home, the committee decided to sponsor a garden bazaar to raise money for the upkeep of the place. The organising committee placed an advertisement in the Jewish newspapers, announcing the event and the names of the girls under its present care.

A Mr Sztokman, who originated from Tarnogród, read the advertisement. As a boy he had attended my grandfather's *cheder* and knew my whole family. He, his wife and her parents had lived in Germany the last few years before the war. They had managed to escape to Britain just before the war broke out. He wrote to me saying that he would like me to come to London. I could hardly write English then; yet I managed to write a few words, asking him if he had a wife, as this would make it easier for me to visit.

It did not take long before I received a reply, this time

from Mrs Sztokman. She wrote that she and her husband were both awaiting my visit to London at a convenient time of my choosing. 'Furthermore,' she wrote, 'we want to let you know that your visit will be of very great significance to us and to many of our friends who will also be here. We are quite convinced that you will have a most horrendous story to tell us of how you managed to survive. We hope that you will also bring us some good news about our dear families in Tarnogród.'

Sadly, they were still hoping for stories of miraculous survivals. I delayed that first visit for a week, reluctant to bring them news of what had happened in Tarnogród and in all of Poland. I knew that anyone who had not been present could not yet comprehend or believe the horrors which had taken place.

After a week elapsed, the urge to see people from my home town overcame my reluctance, and I travelled to the Sztokmans in London. I received a royal welcome from the hosts and all their friends. As Mrs Sztokman had said in her letter, her friends gathered to meet me, hoping to get information about the relatives they had left behind in Poland.

During the meal, I unfolded the sad story of my life on the run from the Nazis. News of the scale of the massacres outside the concentration camps was not yet common knowledge. The story I now told them shattered any hope they may still have harboured for the survival of some of their families. Sadness and disbelief that such things could have happened left the Sztokmans and their friends speechless. Then tears began flowing from everyone's eyes, including mine. It was at this time that I really cried for all those six years that I lived a life of make-believe.

Before the visitors left, they tried to give me some money, but I declined to take any. It was not so much pride but the desire to earn my own money that made me refuse their offers. Also, I could not plan my future by taking handouts, for eventually those would stop. I had to rely on myself and not on others.

Mr Sztokman began making inquiries for me about any surviving relatives I may have had in Britain. A few days later, he came home with very good news.

'Your grandfather's cousin is here in London,' he said. 'He left Poland on a business trip just before the war.'

I became very excited. 'Can it really be true? A relative of mine survived the Holocaust?'

It was difficult to contain my excitement. Soon, I would come face to face with my own flesh and blood. With very great enthusiasm and very little patience, I awaited this forthcoming meeting. Yet somewhere in the back of my mind, I did not really believe that it could be true.

Thankfully, my relative, Meir Schwartz, turned out to be quite real. The last time he visited us in Tarnogród, I had still been very young, and I could not remember him too well. But my heart almost stopped when I saw him. He looked so much like my grandfather that I thought I was seeing a ghost.

I felt so sorry for that old man that I had to unfold the sad news about his lost family to him too. He began to cry, for he had lost his wife and all his children. Being young, I managed to console him; I reminded him that everyone in his family had been good and innocent, like my own family, and that they must all now be in Heaven.

I was tremendously happy to tell my relative that I had remained observant while living among Christians. I also told him that although I could not observe all the *mitzvos* during those dreadful times, I intended to observe them from then on. I could see that he was suddenly happier than when we first met. Now he had a mission: to find an observant boy for me to marry.

35. A Shidduch

At last, the day of the garden bazaar, sponsored by the refugee committee, arrived. The hostel, which was always kept spotless, had been cleaned even more thoroughly than usual. I volunteered to cut the grass as I was good at tending gardens. Miss Pearlman, who had noted my 'green fingers', indulged me affectionately. After mowing the lawn, I cut fresh flowers and arranged them in vases. The premises throughout had a festive look.

We had also taken extra care in grooming ourselves, ironing our dresses and curling our hair. We wanted to look special, for we had been told that the guests would photograph us; they wanted to show their families pictures of us, those miraculous survivors. We felt very important, and our faces shone with happiness.

We all helped set up wooden tables and laid out the refreshments brought in from London.

At last, the people began to arrive. After shaking the hand of each one of us, they looked us up and down as if we had come from a different planet. We felt different, too. We were all well aware that we had survived only by the grace of Heaven. I looked out of a window at the flowers in the garden and felt as if I were in *Gan Eden*, paradise. I praised *Hashem* for allowing me to breathe that sweet air and walk among friends once more.

I was awakened from my reveries by the voice of our sweet matron. 'Come along, all of you,' she said. 'Everyone is eager to take pictures of you now.'

We all followed her obediently down the corridor, where the visitors were already waiting with their cameras ready. I felt very tall and happy as we lined up for the photographs. We were now the stars, and everyone looked at us with true love. They could not take their eyes off us. They told us over and over how much they admired our courage, our heroism, our ability to withstand what we had withstood.

'May the Lord bless you forever more,' they said to us all, and then they began approaching individual girls with invitations to visit them in London.

A sudden sense that I was being stared at made me look up. Miss Pearlman, in earnest conversation with two gentlemen, was pointing in my direction. I wondered why they were talking about me. The mystery was soon resolved when they came over and introduced themselves as my very own uncles.

I stared at them with disbelief. I wondered how my father's brothers from as far off as Uruguay had discovered not only that I was alive but also that I was in England.

'Are you Uncle Jacob and Uncle Meilich?' I asked them. 'Have you come all the way from Uruguay?'

'We're from London,' they told me. 'We're originally from Germany and Holland, and we're your late mother's uncles and not your father's brothers.'

I was stunned by this revelation and suspected that

they were maybe making this up. However, when they mentioned my dear parents' names I believed them.

'I now have relatives, true relatives,' I told the others, and I could see that they were envious of me. How I wished I could have shared my uncles with them all. Perhaps I should not have told the other girls about my good fortune. They did not yet know if any of their relatives had survived, and there I was, boasting that I had found some. Nevertheless, I could see they were happy for me, because we had become as close as sisters.

My great-uncles and I sat in front of a food-laden table as I related some of the experiences I had endured. Had I known that Uncle Aussenberg had lost three children in the Holocaust, I would have been more careful about what I said. But I spoke blithely, entranced with my good luck at having been found by relatives and with the happy notion that they had all escaped. By the time I realised the truth, it was too late to hold back. However, after learning about my experiences, they forgot their own sorrows and managed to console me, saying that I was still young and that I would still have a very happy life one day. As lucky as I then felt, it was still hard to visualise a happy future. I continued to visit them and their families many times.

Several months later, our hostel was moved from Kings Langley to Brixton in London. This hostel was not run as an observant institution, and I decided to leave.

I soon found employment as an apprentice dressmaker. The wages were meagre, but I regained my self-confidence and resolved to make my own way in more observant surroundings. I began to spend some weekends with my relatives who managed to locate the address of my uncle in Palestine. In his first correspondence, he expressed his delight at hearing that I was not among the youngsters who were killed in the road accident in Föhrenwald on the way from Munich. I wrote back saying that I hoped to meet him and his family one day. This dream came true several years later when I travelled to *Eretz Yisrael* to visit them.

I greatly rejoiced to be in a house with a real uncle and aunt, and it was comforting to see that they were observant, just like we were at home. It did not take long before I found more relatives in London. A few of my mother's cousins had managed to escape just before the war started. Although they were no substitute for my immediate family, I was glad to have them.

It was time for me to prepare myself for the future. As before, I had to plan it myself. It was now 1946, and I was still too young and too inexperienced to have thoughts of marriage. For a few years, I lived in hostels with many other girls. Finally, I left to fend for myself. I could not afford my own apartment, so I rented rooms from observant families. I changed my lodgings many times to try to better myself, and I was not always treated in the best way. I often went hungry as it was not always easy for me to manage on my insubstantial wages.

But the freedom I began to feel compensated for any shortcomings. I started cooking for myself and learned how to keep house. It was after I had learned to keep house that loneliness began to plague me. I began thinking about marriage.

Mr Sztokman informed me one day that he had heard about some boys from Tarnogród who were now learning in Eitz Chaim, a *yeshiva* in the East End of London. Although it was hard to believe that there were any more survivors from my home town, I travelled from Kings Langley to see for myself. I found out that I indeed knew the boys' families quite well, although I did not recognise the boys themselves. They had survived the war in Siberia.

It did not take very long before Meir Schwartz, my grandfather's cousin, introduced me to Meir Kacenberg, to whom I became engaged shortly afterwards. Meir had survived the war in Siberia, where life was extremely difficult; but his parents had not survived the ordeal. Both Meir and I knew quite well that it would not be so easy for us to arrange everything for ourselves in preparation for our forthcoming wedding. However, I realised that worry alone would bring us nowhere and that a lot of realistic thinking was needed by both of us. Now that at last *Hashem* had helped us find each other, we both prayed that He would assist us once more.

Since Meir's English was not yet fluent, it was not easy for him to find employment; we realised that our engagement would not result in marriage for quite a while. We were also greatly saddened that Mr Schwartz passed away so soon after introducing us and did not live long enough to be at our wedding.

It was on February 20, 1949, that Meir and I

eventually got married, and we have never looked back. Both my husband and I are very grateful that we have managed, with *Hashem*'s help, to raise five children who all live a life of which even our forefathers would have been proud.

At about the time of my wedding, my beloved cat Malach, who had stayed by my side during my most desperate situations for six awful years, vanished. I never saw her again. I never managed to have a photograph taken of her. But I will keep her image in my mind for as long as I live.

My thoughts often go back to those tragic years of suffering, and the memories of my beloved Malach return with vivid clarity and retrospective amazement. There is no doubt in my mind that this was no ordinary cat. Time and again, Malach showed an uncanny ability to warn me of danger and extricate me from it. Very often, her very presence seemed to emanate a shield of protection between me and my tormentors. Moreover, even when we became separated from each other by great distances, Malach would somehow reappear at my side in defiance of all logical explanation. And of course, there is the inexplicable phenomenon that in all the years of our companionship I never saw Malach eat or drink. As strange as it may sound, I am convinced that Malach was indeed a true *malach*, a guardian angel sent by Heaven to protect me and guide me through the inferno that destroyed my family, my town and six million of my people.

Why did I, of all people, deserve my own guardian

angel? I do not know. Certainly, I was no more deserving than countless thousands of others who perished. Perhaps it was in the merit of my parents or one of my worthy ancestors whose name and life are perpetuated through my children and grandchildren. Who can fathom the ways of *Hashem*? Certainly not I.

Nevertheless, no matter in whose merit I was granted this divine shield, I do not cease to praise and thank *Hashem* for His infinite kindness. Every time I see my children and grandchildren, all of them living embodiments of the holy Torah, I want to call out to my dear parents in *Gan Eden*, 'Look! These are your grandchildren! Be proud, because your lifelong devotion to the Torah and your selfless love for your children are reflected in the shining faces of your grandchildren. Through them and your future generations, you will continue to live forever.'

Author's father, Yitzchok
Kacenberg, 1932

Author's mother,
Frimche Kacenberg,
with baby sister
Devorah, 1933

Mala Kacenberg, during her
engagement, 1948

Mr and Mrs Kacenberg, 1994

Mala at the Perlmutts' Christmas party in the hotel where she was employed (Mala standing second row far left)

Mala and other survivors at Feldafing holiday camp

Mala and other refugees at a hostel at Kings
Langley near Watford

Mala and Meir during their engagement, 1948

Glossary

Appell: roll call
Belzer Shtiebl: small informal synagogue
bentch: to bless
berachah: a form of blessing, often recited before eating
broit: bread
challos: *Shabbos* loaves
Chanukah: Festival of Lights
chassid: adherent of *chassidus*
chassidus: Jewish pietist movement
cheder: elementary Torah school
daven: to pray
Einsatzgruppen: Nazi extermination troops
Eretz Yisrael: The 'Land of Israel', the Jewish biblical
  homeland
Erev Rosh Hashanah: Jewish New Year's Eve
Gan Eden: the Garden of Eden, paradise
Gemeinde: administrative building
gutten morgen: good morning [Yiddish]
guten Morgen: good morning [German]
Hashem: Hebrew informal term for God
Herrenvolk: Hitler's 'master race'
kalle: bride
kapitlach Tehillim: chapters of Psalms
Kiddush: sanctification of *Shabbos* or festivals
Magen David: Star of David

malach: angel

mazel tov: congratulations

melamed: teacher

minyan: quorum of ten

mitzvos: Torah commandments

Rosh Hashanah: Jewish New Year

Selichos: penitential prayers

shidduch: a marriage match

shul: synagogue

siddur: prayer book

talmid chacham: learned Torah scholar

tefillos: prayers

treif: unkosher

Vidui: confession

yeshivah: Torah school

Yom Kippur: Jewish Day of Atonement

Yom Tov: a Jewish holiday

zchus: merit

Zeidy: informal term for grandfather

Ribono Shel Olam, helf shoin mir,
Ich hof tzi kainem nisht, nor tzi dir,
Die hilf is doch fin kainem nisht, nor fin dir,
Ribono Shel Olam, helf shoin mir.
Master of the Universe, please help me,
Please help me, I pray to no one but to You,
Help comes from no one but from You,
Master of the Universe, please help me.

Yiddish prayer taught to Mala by her mother